ISBN 978-1-334-51794-5
PIBN 10577215

PHILOLOGICAL

INQUIRIES.

PART THE THIRD.

Ja.s Stuart Esq.r del. W.m Sharp sculp.t

PHILOLOGICAL INQUIRIES

IN

THREE PARTS

BY

IAMES HARRIS ESQ.

PART III.

LONDON,

Printed for C. NOURSE, in the Strand.

MDCCLXXXI.

PHILOLOGICAL INQUIRIES.

PART THE THIRD.

CHAPTER I.

Design of the whole—Limits and Extent of THE MIDDLE AGE—THREE CLASSES *of Men, during that interval, conspicuous;* THE BYZANTINE GREEKS; THE SARACENS *or* ARABIANS; *and* THE LATINS *or* FRANKS, *Inhabitants of Western Europe—Each Class in the following Chapters considered apart.*

WHEN THE MAGNITUDE OF THE ROMAN EMPIRE grew *enormous*, and there were *two* imperial Cities, ROME and CONSTANTINOPLE, then that happened, Ch. I.

P. III. pened; which was natural; out of *one* *Empire* it became *two*, distinguished by the different names of the WESTERN, and the EASTERN.

THE WESTERN EMPIRE soon sunk. So early as in the *fifth* Century*, ROME, once the Mistress of Nations, beheld herself at the feet of a *Gothic* Sovereign. THE EASTERN EMPIRE lasted many Centuries

---

* About the year of Christ 475, *Augustulus* was compelled to abdicate the *Western Empire* by *Odoacer*, King of the *Heruli*. As *Augustulus* was the last *Roman*, who possest the Imperial Dignity at *Rome*, and as the Dominion both of *Rome* and *Italy* soon after past into the hands of *Theodoric the Goth*, it has been justly said, that *then* terminated *the Roman Empire in the West*.

During these wretched times, ROME had been sacked not long before by *Alaric*, as it was a second time (about the middle of the sixth Century) by *Totila*; after which events the *Roman* Name and Authority were so far sunk, that early in the seventh Century they ceased *to speak Latin*, even in *Rome* itself. See Blair's Chronology.

turies longer, and, tho' often impaired by *external* Enemies, and weakened as often by *internal* Factions, yet still it retained traces of its *antient* Splendor, resembling in the language of *Virgil* some fair, but faded flower, Ch. I.

Cui neque fulgor adhuc, necdum sua forma recessit. VIRG.

AT length, after various plunges and various escapes, it was totally annihilated in the *fifteenth* Century by the victorious arms of *Mahomet the Great* *.

---

* See the various Histories of the *Turkish* Empire. *The unfortunate Greeks*, at this period, when, to resist such an Enemy as the Turks, they should have been firmly combined, were never so miserably distracted. An *union with the Church of Rome* was at the time projected. The *Greeks*, who favoured it, imputed their Calamities to their *Not-uniting*; those, who opposed it, to their *Uniting*. Between the two Factions all was lost, and *Constantinople* taken in the year 1453.

THE

P. III.

THE INTERVAL BETWEEN THE FALL OF THESE TWO EMPIRES (the *Weſtern* or *Latin* in the *fifth* Century, the *Eaſtern* or *Grecian* in the *fifteenth)* making a ſpace of near a thouſand years, *conſtitutes* what we call THE MIDDLE AGE.

DOMINION paſt during this interval into the hands of rude, illiterate men; men, who conquered more by *multitude*, than by *military ſkill*; and who, having little or no taſte either for Sciences or Arts, naturally deſpiſed thoſe things, from which they had reaped no advantage.

THIS was the age of Monkery and Legends; of *Leonine* Verſes*, (that is of *bad Latin put into rhime*;) of *Projects to decide Truth* by Plough-ſhares and Bat-

* See below, Chap. XI.

toons;

toons*; of *Crusades* to conquer Infidels, and

Ch. I.

* This alludes to the two methods of TRIAL, much practised in those dark times, the Trial by ORDEAL, and that by DUEL.

Heated Plough-shares were often employed in Trials by ORDEAL, and 'tis remarkable that express mention is made of this absurd method of *Purgation by Fire*, even in the *Antigene of Sophocles*. The Messenger there says, in order to justify himself and his Companions—

> Ἦμεν δ᾽ ἕτοιμοι καὶ μύδρους αἴρειν χεροῖν,
> Καὶ πῦρ διέρπειν, καὶ θεοὺς ὁρκωμοτεῖν,
> Τὸ μήτε δρᾶσαι, μήτε, κ. τ. λ.

> *Ready we were with both our hands* TO LIFT
> THE GLOWING MASS; *or slowly* CROSS THE FIRE,
> *And by the Gods to swear, we neither did*
> *The Deed, nor knew, &c.* Antig. v. 270.

This carries up the Practice to the time of *Eteocles* and *Polynices*, before the *Trojan* War.

Perhaps the Poet, by the incidental mention of so strange a Custom, intended to characterise the manners of a *ruder* age; an age, widely different from *his own*, which was an Age of Science and Philosophical Disquisition.

R As

P. III. and extirpate Heretics; of Princes *deposed*,

As to *Trials by* BATTLE, they were either before *the Earl Marshal*, or *the Judges of Westminster Hall.* If before the Earl Marshal, they were upon accusations of Treason or other capital Crimes, and the Parties were usually of high and noble rank. If before the Judges of Westminster Hall, the Cause was often of inferior sort, as well as the Parties litigating.

Hence the Combats differed in their Ends. That before the Earl Marshal was *Victory*, often attended with *slaughter*; that before the Judges was *Victory alone*, with no such consequence.

The Weapons too differed, as well as the Ends. The Weapons before *the Earl Marshal* were a long Sword, a short Sword, and a Dagger: that before *the Judges* was a *Battoon* above mentioned, called in barbarous Latin *Druncus*, but in words more intelligible *Fustis teres*.

So late as the reign of *Queen Elizabeth* an instance occurs of this Trial being insisted upon. But that wise Princess, tho' she permitted the previous forms, I mean that of the Lists being inclosed, of the Judges taking their seats there, of the Champions making their appearance, &c. (*Forms*, which perhaps could not *legally* be prevented) had too much sense to permit so foolish a decision. She compelled the Parties to to a compromise, by the Plaintiff's taking an equivalent in money for his claim, and making in consequence a voluntary default.

Wyvil, Bishop of Salisbury, in the reign of *Edward the Third,* recurred to *Trial by* BATTLE in a dispute with the Earl of Salisbury, and ordered public Prayers thro' his Diocese for the success of his Champion, till the matter, by the King's authority, was compromised.

But notwithstanding this Bishop's Conduct, 'twas A PRACTICE which THE CHURCH *disapproved,* and wisely, as well as humanely endeavoured to prevent. TRUCULENTUM MOREM *in omni ævo acriter insectarunt* THEOLOGI, *præ aliis Agobardus, et plurimo Canone* IPSA ECCLESSIA. See *Spelman,* under the words *Campus, Campsius,* and *Campio.*

I must not omit that there is a complete History of such a *Duel,* recorded by *Walsingham,* in the reign of *Richard the Second,* between *Aneslee* a Knight, and *Karryngton* an Esquire. *Karryngton* was accused by the other of Treason, for selling a Castle to the *French,* and, being defeated in the Combat, died the next day raving mad. *Walsingham*'s Narrative is curious and exact, but their Weapons differed from those above mentioned, for they first fought with *Lances,* then with *Swords,* and lastly with *Daggers.* *Walsing. Histor.* p. 237.

P. III. by one, who had no Armies, and who did not even wear a sword *.

DIFFERENT Portions of this *Age* have been distinguished by different descriptions; such as *Sæculum Monotheleticum*, *Sæculum Eiconoclasticum*, *Sæculum Obscurum*, *Sæculum Ferreum*, *Sæculum Hildibrandinum*,

* Such was Pope *Innocent the third*, who, besides his Crusades to extirpate Heretics by Armies *not his own*, excommunicated *Philip*, King of France; *Alphonso*, King of Leon; *Raimond*, Earl of Toulouse; and *John*, King of England.

Nor is this wonderful, when we view *in his own Language* the Opinion he had of his own Station and Authority.

I am placed (says he) IN THE MIDDLE, *between* GOD *and* MAN, ON THIS SIDE *God*, *but* BEYOND *Man*; *nay I am greater than* MAN, *as I can judge of all Men, but can be judged by no one.* *Sum enim inter* DEUM *et* HOMINEM MEDIUS *constitutus, citra Deum sed ultra Hominem; imò major Homine, qui de omnibus judicem, a nemine vero judicari possim.* Innocen III. *Serm.* 2. *in Historiâ Transubstantionis Joannis Cosin. Episcop. Dunelm. Lond.* 1675. See also *all the Church Histories of this Period.*

num, &c. ſtrange names it muſt be con- Ch. I.
feſt, ſome more obvious, others leſs ſo, yet none tending to furniſh us with any high, or promiſing Ideas *.

AND yet we muſt aknowledge for the honour of *Humanity*, and of its GREAT and DIVINE AUTHOR, who *never* forſakes it, that ſome ſparks of *Intellect* were *at all times* viſible, thro' the whole of this dark and dreary Period. 'Tis *here* we muſt look for the TASTE and LITERATURE OF THE TIMES.

THE few, who were *enlightened*, when Arts and Sciences were thus *obſcured*, may be ſaid to have *happily maintained the Continuity of Knowlege*; to have been (if I may uſe the expreſſion) like the *Twilight* of a

* Thoſe, who would be farther informed concerning theſe *Sæcula*, may, among other authors, conſult two very learned ones, CAVE in his *Hiſtoria Literaria*, and MOSHEIM in his *Eccleſiaſtical Hiſtory*.

P. III. Summer's Night; that auſpicious Gleam between the ſetting and the riſing Sun, which, tho' it cannot retain the Luſtre of the Day, helps at leaſt to ſave us from the *Totality* of Darkneſs.

A curſory Diſquiſition, illuſtrated by a few ſelect Inſtances, will conſtitute the Subject of the preſent Eſſay; and theſe Inſtances we ſhall bring from among THREE CLASSES OF MEN, who had each a large ſhare in the tranſactions of thoſe times; from THE BYZANTINE GREEKS, from THE ARABIANS OR SARACENS, and from *the Inhabitants of Weſtern Europe*, at that time called THE LATINS. We ſhall give Precedence, as we think they merit it, to the GREEKS OF CONSTANTINOPLE, altho' it is not always eaſy to preſerve an *exact* Chronology, becauſe in each of theſe three Claſſes many eminent men were contemporary.

CHAP.

CHAP. II.

Concerning the first Class, THE BYZANTINE GREEKS — SIMPLICIUS — AMMONIUS — PHILOPONUS — *Fate of the fine Library at Alexandria.*

SIMPLICIUS and AMMONIUS were *Greek* Authors, who flouriſhed at ATHENS during the ſixth Century; for *Athens*, long after her Trophies at *Marathon*, long after her *political Sovereignty* was no more, ſtill maintained her Empire in *Philoſophy* and the *fine Arts**. Ch. II.

Philoſophy indeed, when theſe Authors wrote, was ſinking apace. The *Stoic Syſtem*, and even the *Stoic Writings* were the greater part of them loſt†. Other

---

* See below, Chap. III.

† See *Philoſoph. Arrangements*, p. 253.

Sects had ſhared the ſame fate. None ſubſiſted but *the Platonic*, and *the Peripatetic*; which, being both derived from a common ſource (that is to ſay, *the Pythagorean*) were at this period *blended*, and commonly cultivated by the *ſame* Perſons.

Simplicius and Ammonius, being bred in this School, and well initiated in its Principles, found no reaſon, from their education, to make Syſtems *for themſelves*; a practice, referable *ſometimes* to real Genius, but *more often* to not knowing, *what others have invented before*.

Conscious therefore they could not excel their great Predeceſſors, they thought, like many others, that the *Commenting* of their Works was doing mankind the moſt eſſential Service.

'Twas this, which gave riſe, long before *their* time, to that Tribe of Com-

MENTATORS, who, in the perſon of *Andronicus the Rhodian*, began under *Auguſtus*, and who continued, for ages after, in an orderly ſucceſſion. Ch. II.

SIMPLICIUS wrote a variety of Comments upon different parts of *Ariſtotle*; but his *Comment upon the Phyſics* is peculiarly valuable, as it is filled with quotations from *Anaxagoras*, *Democritus*, *Parmenides*, and *other* Philoſophers, who flouriſhed ſo early, as before the time of *Ariſtotle*, and whoſe fragments many of them are not to be found elſe-where.

As this *Compilation* muſt have been the reſult of *extenſive Reading*, we may juſtly diſtinguiſh him by the title of a *learned* Commentator *.

---

* For a fuller and more accurate account of SIMPLICIUS ſee *Fabricii Biblioth. Græc.* Tom. VIII. p. 620, &c.

AMMONIUS

P. III.

AMMONIUS wrote *Comments* on the first and second Tracts of *Aristotle's Logic*, as likewise upon *the Introductory Discourse* of the Philosopher *Porphyry*. His *manner* of writing is orderly; his stile *clear* and *copious*; copious in its better sense, by leaving nothing unexpl ined, not copious by perplexing us with tiresome Tautology.

To those, who wish for a taste of this Literature, I know no Author, who better merits perusal. THE PREFACE to his *Comment on Porphyry* is a curious account of *Philosophy* under its many and different *Definitions*, every one of which he explaines with perspicuity, and precision. THE PREFACE to his *Comment on the Predicaments* gives us an ingenius *Plan of Critical Scrutiny*; in other words furnishes us with *a suite of leading Queries*, by which, before we read a Book, we may learn *what it is*, and judge, when

when analyzed, if it be a *legitimate* Composition*. Ch. II.

When things change by uninterrupted *Continuity*, as (to use an idea already suggested) the splendor of the Day to the darkness of the Night, 'tis hard to decide precisely, where the one concludes, and the other commences. By parity of reasoning 'tis difficult to determine, *to what age* we shall *adjudge* the two Philosophers just mentioned; whether to the Commencement of a *baser* age, or rather (if we regard their merit) to the Conclusion of a *purer*. If we arrange them with the Conclusion, 'tis, as *Brutus* and *Cassius* were called *the last of the Romans*†.

We can have less doubt about the disciple of *Ammonius*, John the Grammarian,

* See *Fabr. Biblioth. Græc.* T. IV. p. 161.
† See *Tacit. Annal.* IV. 34.

MARIAN,

P. III. MARIAN, called PHILOPONUS from his love of labour. 'Twas his misfortune to live during the time of *Mahomet*, and to see *Alexandria* taken by the Arms of one of his immediate Successors. What past there on this occasion with regard to *the Library*, tho' recorded in modern Books, is too curious to be omitted here. I translate it from the accurate version of *Abulpharagius's History*, made by that able Orientalist, *Pococke*.

" WHEN *Alexandria* was taken by the
" *Mahometans*, AMRUS, their Commander,
" found there PHILOPONUS, whose con-
" versation highly pleased him, as *Amrus*
" was a lover of Letters, and *Philoponus*
" a learned Man. On a certain day *Phi-*
" *loponus* said to him: *You have visited*
" *all the Repositories or Public Warehouses*
" *in Alexandria, and you have sealed up*
" *things of every sort, that are found*
" *there. As to those things, that may be*
" *useful*

" *useful to you, I presume to say nothing;* " *but as to things of no service to* You, " *some of them perhaps may be more suitable* " *to* Me. *Amrus* said to him: *And what* " *is it you want? The Philosophical Books* " (replied he) *preserved in the Royal Li-* " *braries. This,* says *Amrus, is a request,* " *upon which I cannot decide. You desire* " *a thing, where I can issue no orders,* " *till I have leave from* Omar, *the Com-* " *mander of the Faithful.* Letters were " accordingly written to *Omar*, inform- " ing him of what *Philoponus* had said, " and an Answer was returned by Omar " to the following purport.—" *As to the* " *Books, of which you have made mention,* " *if there be contained in them, what ac-* " *cords with the Book of God* (meaning " the Alcoran) *there is without them,* " *in the Book of God, all that is sufficient.* " *But if there be any thing in them re-* " *pugnant to that Book, we in no respect* " *want them. Order them therefore to be* " *all*

" *all destroyed:* *Amrus* upon this ordered
" them to be dispersed thro' the Baths of
" *Alexandria*, and to be there burnt in
" making the Baths warm. After this
" manner, in the space of six months,
" they were all consumed."

THE Historian, having related the Story, adds from his own feelings, HEAR WHAT WAS DONE, AND WONDER*.

THUS ended this noble Library; and thus began, if it did not begin sooner, *the Age of Barbarity and Ignorance.*

---

* Vid. *Abulpharagii Dynastiar.* p. 114. *Oxon:* 1663.

The Reader will *here* observe, that in the many Quotations, which we shall hereafter make from *Abulpharagius*, we shall *always* quote from the same Edition; that is, from the *Latin Version* of the learned *Pocock*, subjoined to the *original Arabic.*

CHAP.

CHAP. III.

Digression to a short Historical Account of ATHENS, *from the time of her* Persian *Triumphs, to that of her becoming subject to the* Turks—*Sketch, during this long interval, of her Political and Literary State; of her Philosophers; of her Gymnasia; of her good and bad Fortune,* &c. &c.—*Manners of the present Inhabitants—Olives and Honey.*

HAVING mentioned ATHENS, I hope that celebrated City will justify a Digression, and the more so, as that Digression will terminate in Events, which belong to *the very Age*, of which we are now writing. But 'tis expedient to deduce matters from a much earlier period. Ch.III.

WHEN the *Athenians* had delivered themselves from the tyranny of PISISTRATUS, and after this had defeated the vast

Efforts

P. III. Efforts of the *Persians*, and that against two successive Invaders, DARIUS and XERXES, they may be considered as at the summit of their *national* Glory. For more than half a century afterwards they maintained, without controul, *the Sovereignty of Greece* *.

As their *Taste* was naturally good, *Arts* of every kind soon rose among them, and flourished. Valour had given them Reputation; Reputation gave them an Ascendant; and that Ascendant produced a Security, which left their minds at ease, and gave them leisure to cultivate every thing liberal, or elegant †.

'TWAS

* For these *Historical Facts* consult the *antient* and *modern Authors* of *Grecian History*.

† 'Twas in a similar period of *Triumph*, after a formidable Adversary had been crushed, that *the Romans* began to cultivate a more refined and polished Literature.

——*post*

'Twas then that Pericles adorned the City with Temples, Theatres, and other beautiful public Buildings. Phidias, the great Sculptor, was employed as his Architect, who, when he had erected Edifices, adorned them himself, and added *Statues* and Basso-relievo's, the admiration of every beholder*. 'Twas then that Polygnotus and Myro painted; that Sophocles and Euripides wrote; and not long after, that they saw *the divine* Socrates. Ch.III.

Human affairs are by nature prone to change, and states as well as individuals

——*post Punica bella* QUIETUS, *quærere cœpit,*
Quid Sophocles, et Thespis, et Æschylus utile ferrent.
Horat. Ep. II. L. II. v. 162.

See the Note from a Greek MS. subjoined to the third Edition of my First Volume, p. 361, where the Progress of Arts and Sciences, from their Dawn to their Meridian, is elegantly and philosophically exhibited.

* See *Plutarch*'s Life of *Pericles*, p. 350, 351, 352, 353, 354. in the Quarto *Greek* Edition of *Bryan*, Vol. I. and *Stuart's Antiquities of Athens.*

P. III. are born to decay. Jealousy and Ambition insensibly fomented wars, and Success in these wars, as in others, was often *various*. The *military* strength of the ATHENIANS was first impaired by the LACEDÆMONIANS; after that, it was again humiliated, under EPAMINONDAS, by the *Thebans*; and last of all it was wholly crushed by *the Macedonian*, PHILIP*.

BUT tho' their *political* Sovereignty was lost, yet, happily for Mankind, their *Love* of LITERATURE and ARTS did not sink along with it.

JUST at the close of their *Golden Days of Empire* flourished XENOPHON and PLATO, the disciples of SOCRATES, and from *Plato* descended that Race of Philosophers, called *the old Academy* †.

---

* See, as before, the several Histories of *Greece*.

† See *Cic. de Fin.* L. V. and *Academ.* L. I. s. 5. p. 21. *Edit. Davisii.*

ARIS-

ARISTOTLE, who was *Plato*'s disciple, may be said, not to have invented *a new* Philosophy, but rather to have tempered the sublime, and rapturous mysteries of his master with Method, *Order*, and a stricter Mode of reasoning *. Ch. III.

ZENO, who was himself also educated in the principles of *Platonism*, only differed from *Plato* in the *comparative* Estimate of things, allowing nothing to be *intrinsically good but* VIRTUE, nothing *intrinsically bad but* VICE, and considering all other things to be *in themselves indifferent* †.

He too and *Aristotle* accurately cultivated *Logic*, but in *different* ways; for

* See *Hermes*, p. 421.

† See *Cicer. de Fin.* L. III. s. 7. 8. 16. — the beginning of the *Enchiridion of Epictetus*, Τῶν ὄντων τὰ μὲν ἐφ' ἡμῖν, κ. τ. λ. *Diogen. Laert. in vitâ Zenon.* L. VII. s. 102.

P. III. *Aristotle* chiefly dwelt upon the *simple* Syllogism; *Zeno* upon that which is derived out of it, the *Compound* or *Hypothetic*. Both too, as well as other Philosophers, cultivated *Rhetoric* along with *Logic*; holding a knowlege in *both* to be requisite for those, who think of addressing mankind with all the efficacy of *Persuasion*. ZENO elegantly illustrated the force of these *two* powers by a Simile, taken from the Hand: the *close* power of *Logic* he compared to the *Fist*, or *Hand comprest*; the *diffuse* power of *Logic*, to the *Palm*, or *Hand open* *.

I shall

---

* ZENO *quidem ille, a quo disciplina Stoicorum est*, MANU *demonstrare solebat, quid inter has artes* [Dialecticam scil. et Eloquentiam] *interesset. Nam, cum compresserat digitos*, PUGNUM *que fecerat*, DIALECTICAM *aiebat ejusmodi esse: cum autem diduxerat, et manum dilataverat*, PALMÆ *illius similem* ELOQUENTIAM *esse* dicebat. *Cicer. Orator.* s. 113.

Both *Peripatetics* and *Stoics* wrote Tracts of *Rhetoric* as well as *Logic*. The RHETORIC of *Aristotle* is perhaps

I ſhall mention but *two* Sects more, *the New Academy*, and *the Epicurean*. Ch. III.

The *New Academy*, ſo called from *the Old Academy*, (the name given to the School of *Plato*) was founded by Arcesilas, and ably maintained by Carneades. From a miſtaken imitation of the great parent of *Philoſophy*, *Socrates*, (particularly as he appears in the Dialogues of *Plato*) becauſe *Socrates* doubted *ſome* things, therefore *Arceſilas* and *Carneades* doubted *all**.

haps one of the moſt valuable Remains of Antiquity, and deſervedly worth ſtudying, be it for *Speculation* or *Practice*.

As for the Rhetoric of the *Stoics*, there is extant, among the *Latin* Rhetoricians, publiſhed in a thin *Quarto* by *Plantin* at *Paris*, an. 1599, a Tract by *Sulpitius Victor*, called *Inſtitutiones Oratoriæ*, wherein he has this Expreſſion at the beginning—Zenonis *præcepta maximè perſecutus*. See p. 240—alſo p. 247, 264, of the ſaid Treatiſe.

* Vid. Cic. Academ. L. I. ſ. 13. p. 48. Edit. Dav. *Itaque Arceſilas negabat eſſe quicquam*, &c.

P. III.

EPICURUS drew from another source; DEMOCRITUS had taught him *Atoms* and *a Void*: by the *fortuitous concourse of Atoms* he fancied he could *form a World*, while by a *feigned* Veneration he complimented away his GODS, and totally denied their *Providential Care*, lest the *Trouble* of it should impair their *uninterrupted* State of Bliss. VIRTUE he recommended, tho' *not* for the sake of *Virtue*, but *Pleasure*; PLEASURE, according to him, being *our chief* and *sovereign Good*. It must be confest however, that, tho' his Principles were *erroneous* and even *bad*, never was a Man more *temperate* and *humane*; never was a Man more beloved by his Friends, or more cordially attached to them in affectionate esteem *.

* See *Diogen. Laert.* L. X. s. 9, &c where an ample Detail is given of *Epicurus*, his Friends, his last Will, and his Death, all tending to establish his *Amiable* Character, however *erroneous* and *blameable* his Doctrines.

WE

We have already mentioned the alliance between *Philoſophy* and *Rhetoric*. This cannot be thought wonderful, if *Rhetoric* be the Art, by which men are *perſuaded*, and if *Men* cannot be perſuaded, without a knowlege of *Human Nature*: for what, but PHILOSOPHY, can procure us *this knowlege*?

'TWAS for this reaſon the ableſt *Greek Philoſophers* not only taught (as we hinted before) but wrote alſo Treatiſes upon *Rhetoric*. They had a farther inducement, and that was the *intrinſic beauty of their Language*, as it was then ſpoken among the learned and polite. They would have been aſhamed to have delivered *Philoſophy*, as it has been too often delivered ſince, in Compoſitions as clumſy, as the common Dialect of the mere Vulgar.

THE ſame *Love of Elegance*, which made them attend to their STILE, made

P. III. them attend even to the PLACES, where their Philoſophy was taught.

Plato delivered his Lectures in a Place ſhaded with Groves, on the Banks of the River *Iliſſus*; and which, as it once belonged to a perſon called *Academus*, was called, after his name, THE ACADEMY*. *Ariſtotle* choſe another ſpot of a *ſimilar* character, where there were *Trees* and *Shade*; a ſpot called THE LYCÆUM†. *Zeno* taught in a PORTICO or COLONADE, diſtinguiſhed from other buildings of that ſort (of which *the Athenians* had many) by the name of the VARIEGATED PORTICO, the Walls being decorated with *various Paintings of Polygnotus* and *Myro*, two capital Maſters of that tranſcendent

* Vid. *Diog. Laert.* Lib. III. ſ. 7. *Potter's Arch. Græc.* Vol. I. p. 40.

† See *Potter's Arch. Græc.* Vol. I. p. 40.

Period,

Period *. *Epicurus* addreſſed his hearers in thoſe well known *Gardens*, called, after Ch. III.

* Of theſe two Artiſts it appears that *Myro* was *paid*, and that *Polygnotus* painted *gratis*, for which generoſity he had the teſtimony of public Honours. *Plin. N. Hiſt.* L. XXXV. cap. 9. ſect. 35.

We learn from Hiſtory that the Pictures, which adorned this *Portico*, were four; two on *the back part* of it (open to the Colonnade) and a Picture at each end, upon *the right* and *left*.

We learn alſo the Subjects: on one of the ſides a Picture of the *Athenian* and *Lacedæmonian* Armies at *Oenoe* (an *Argive* City) facing each other, and ready to engage: on the back Ground, or middle part of the Portico, the Battle between the *Athenians under Theſeus*, and *the Amazons*: next to that, on the ſame middle, the *Grecian Chiefs*, after the taking of *Troy*, deliberating upon the Violence offered by *Ajax* to *Caſſandra*, *Ajax* himſelf being preſent, together with *Caſſandra* and other Captive *Trojan* women: laſtly, on the other ſide of the Portico oppoſite to the firſt, the triumphant Victory at Marathon, the Barbarians puſhed into the Moraſs, or demoliſhed, while they endeavoured to eſcape to their ſhips; Miltiades and the Greek Leaders being to be known by their Portraits.

P. III. after his own name, THE GARDENS OF EPICURUS.

Some of these *Places* gave names to the *Doctrines*, which were taught there. *Plato*'s PHILOSOPHY took its name of ACADEMIC from *the Academy* †; that of *Zeno* was called THE STOIC, from a *Greek* word, signifying *a Portico* ‡.

As the Portico was large, and the Pictures were only four, these we may suppose must have been large likwise, for 'tis probable they occupied the whole space. *Vid. Pausan. Attic.* Lib. I. c. 15. p. 36. *Edit. Lips.* 1696.

From the painting of this *Portico* to the time of *Honorius*, when it was defaced, stript, and its pictures destroyed*, was an interval of about eight hundred years..

It may merit Inquiry among the curious, *upon what sort of Surface*, and *with what sort of Colours*, Pictures were painted, *that could indure so long.*

† See the Note, next after the following.

‡ Στοὰ, Στωϊκοί.

* *Synes. Epist.* 135.

THE

THE Syſtem indeed of *Ariſtotle* was not denominated from the Place, but was called PERIPATETIC, from the manner in which he taught; *from his walking about*, at the time, *when he diſſerted**. The Term, EPICUREAN PHILOSOPHY, needs no Explanation.

OPEN Air, Shade, Water, and pleaſant Walks ſeem above all things to favour that *Exerciſe*, the beſt ſuited to *Contemplation*, I mean *gentle walking without inducing fatigue*. The many agreeable Walks in and about OXFORD may teach my own Countrymen the truth of this aſſertion, and beſt explain how *Horace* lived, while a ſtudent at ATHENS, employed (as he tells us)

* *Qui erant cum Ariſtotele*, PERIPATETICI *dicti ſunt, quia diſputabant* INAMBULANTES *in Lyceo*; *illi autem, qui Platonis inſtituto in* ACADEMIA, *quod eſt alterum gymnaſium, cœtus erant et ſermones habere ſoliti*, E LOCI VOCABULO NOMEN *habuerunt*. Cic. Academ. L. I. c. 4. p. 21, *Edit. Daviſ.*

—*inter*

P. III. —*inter* SILVAS ACADEMI *quærere verum.*

THESE *Places of Public Inſtitution* were called among the *Greeks* by the name of GYMNASIA, in which, whatever that word might have originally meant, were taught all thoſe *Exerciſes*, and all thoſe *Arts*, which tended to cultivate not only THE BODY, but THE MIND. As *Man* was a Being conſiſting of *both*, the *Greeks* could not conſider that Education as complete, in which *both* were not regarded, and *both* properly formed. Hence their *Gymnaſia*, with reference to this *double* End, were adorned with *two Statues*, thoſe of MERCURY and of HERCULES, the *corporeal* Accompliſhments being patronized (as they ſuppoſed) by *the God of Strength*, the *mental* Accompliſhments by the *God of Ingenuity* *.

* Vid. *Athen. Deipnoſ.* L XIII. p. 561. Edit Lugduni, 1657, Fol. Sometimes the *two* Gods were made into *one* Statue. Such compound Statues were called Ἑρμηρακλαι. See *Cic. ad Atticum*, L. I. Epiſt. X.

'TIS

'Tis to be feared, that many Places, *now called Academies*, ſcarce deſerve the name upon this *extenſive* Plan, if the Profeſſors teach no more, than how to dance, fence, and ride upon horſes.

'Twas for the Cultivation of *every liberal Accompliſhment* that Athens was celebrated (as we have ſaid) during many Centuries, long after her *Political* influence was loſt, and at an end.

When Alexander the Great died, *many Tyrants*, like many *Hydras*, immediately ſprung up. Athens then, tho' ſhe ſtill maintained the form of her *antient* Government, was perpetually checked and humiliated by their inſolence. Antipater deſtroyed her *Orators*, and ſhe was *ſacked* by Demetrius *. At length

* See the Writers (antient and modern) of *Grecian* Hiſtory.

ſhe

P. III. ſhe became ſubject to the all-powerful ROMANS, and found the cruel SYLLA her ſevereſt Enemy.

HIS Face (which perhaps indicated his Manners) was of a purple red, intermixed with white. This circumſtance could not eſcape *the witty Athenians:* they deſcribed him in a verſe, and ridiculouſly ſaid,

SYLLA's *face is a Mulberry, ſprinkled with meal* *.

THE Devaſtations and Carnage, which he cauſed ſoon after, gave them too much reaſon to repent their *Sarcaſm.*

---

* The original Verſe is a Trochaïc.

Συκάμινον ἔσθ' ὁ Σύλλας, ἀλφίτῳ πεπασμένον.

Plutarch. in vit. Syllæ, T. III. p 44. *Ed. Bryan*, Quarto.

For his devaſtations of the Groves in the *Academy* and *Lyceum*, his demolition of their fine Buildings, and above all, his cruel maſſacre of the Inhabitants, when he took the City, ſee pages 61, 63, 64, 65 of the ſame Work, in the ſame Edition.

THE

THE civil War between CÆSAR and POMPEY ſoon followed, and their *natural Love of Liberty* made them ſide with *Pompey*. Here again they were unfortunate, for *Cæſar* conquered. But CÆSAR did not treat them like *Sylla*. With that Clemency, which made ſo amiable a part of his character, he diſmiſſed them by a fine alluſion to their illuſtrious Anceſtors, ſaying, *that he ſpared the Living for the ſake of the Dead**.

ANOTHER ſtorm followed ſoon after this, the wars of BRUTUS and CASSIUS with AUGUSTUS and ANTONY. Their Partiality for *Liberty* did not here forſake them: they took part in the conteſt with the two *patriot Romans*, and erected their Statues near their own antient Deliverers, *Harmodius* and *Ariſtogiton*, who had ſlain

* Vid. *Meurſium de Fortunâ Athenarum, in Gronov. Theſaur. Antiquitat. Græcar.* T. V. p. 1745, 1746.

Hip-

P. III. *Hipparchus.* But they were ſtill unhappy, for their Enemies triumphed.

THEY made their peace however with AUGUSTUS, and having met afterwards with different treatment under different Emperors, ſometimes favourable, ſometimes harſh, and never more ſevere than under VESPASIAN, their Oppreſſions were at length relieved by the virtuous NERVA and TRAJAN*.

MANKIND during the interval, which began from NERVA, and which extended to the death of that beſt of Emperors, MARCUS ANTONINUS, felt a reſpite from thoſe evils, which they had ſo ſeverely felt before, and which they felt ſo ſeverely revived under COMMODUS, and his wretched ſucceſſors.

---

* See the ſame Tract, in the ſame Volume of Gronovius's Collection, 1746, 1747.

Ch. III.

ATHENS, during the above golden period, enjoyed more than all others the general felicity, for ſhe found in ADRIAN ſo generous a *Benefactor*, that her citizens could hardly help eſteeming him a *ſecond Founder*. He reſtored their old Privileges; gave them new; repaired their antient Buildings, and added others of his own. MARCUS ANTONINUS, altho' he did not do ſo much, ſtill continued to ſhew them his benevolent attention*.

IF from this period we turn our eyes back, we ſhall find, for Centuries before, that ATHENS was the *place of Education*, not only for *Greeks*, but for *Romans*. 'Twas hither, that HORACE was ſent by his father; 'twas here that CICERO put his ſon MARCUS under CRATIPPUS, one

* See the ſame Author, in the ſame Volume, p. 1748, 1749.

P. III. of the ableſt Philoſophers then belonging to that City *.

The Sects of Philoſophers, which we have already deſcribed, were ſtill exiſting, when St. PAUL came thither. We cannot enough admire the ſuperior Eloquence of that Apoſtle, in his manner of addreſſing ſo intelligent an Audience. We cannot enough admire the ſublimity of his Exordium; the propriety of his mentioning *an Altar*, which he had found there; and his Quotation from ARATUS, one of their well-known Poets †.

NOR was *Athens* only celebrated for the Reſidence of Philoſophers, and the Inſtitution of Youth: Men of rank and

* See *Horat. Epiſt.* II. L. II. v. 43, and the beginning of *Cicero's Offices*, addreſt to his Son—*Quamquam, Marce Fili*, &c.

† ACTS, Ch. xvii. v. 22, &c.

fortune

fortune found pleaſure in a *retreat*, which contributed ſo much to their *liberal* Enjoyment. Ch.III.

The friend and correſpondent of *Cicero*, T. Pomponius, from his long attachment to this City and Country had attained ſuch a perfection in its Arts and Language, that he acquired to himſelf the additional name of Atticus. This great Man may be ſaid to have lived during times of the worſt and crueleſt factions. His youth was ſpent under *Sylla* and *Marius*; the middle of his life during all the ſanguinary ſcenes that followed; and, when he was old, he ſaw the proſcriptions of *Antony* and *Octavius*. Yet tho' *Cicero* and a multitude more of the beſt men periſhed, he had the good fortune to ſurvive every danger. Nor did he ſeek a ſafety for himſelf alone; his Virtue ſo recommended him to the Leaders of every ſide, that he was able to ſave

P. III. not himſelf alone, but the lives and fortunes of many of his friends *.

When we look to this amiable character, we may well ſuppoſe, that it was not merely for amuſement that he choſe to live at *Athens*; but rather that, by reſiding there, he might ſo far realize Philoſophy, as to employ it for the conduct of Life, and not merely for Oſtentation.

Another perſon, during a better period, (that I mean between *Nerva* and *Marcus Antoninus*) was equally celebrated for his affection to this City. By this perſon I mean Herodes Atticus, who acquired the *laſt* name from the ſame

* The Life of this extraordinary man is finely and fully written by *Cornelius Nepos*, a Life well worthy of peruſal. See alſo the large and valuable Collection of *Confidential Letters*, addreſt to him by *Cicero*.

reaſons,

reasons, for which it had formerly been given to *Pomponius* *. Ch. III.

We have remarked already, that Vicissitudes befal both Men and Cities, and changes too often happen from prosperous to adverse. Such was the state of ATHENS under the successors of *Alexander*, and so on from *Sylla* down to the time of *Augustus*. It shared the same hard fate with the *Roman* Empire in general upon the accession of *Commodus*.

AT length, after a certain period, the Barbarians of the North began to pour into the South. *Rome* was taken by ALARIC, and *Athens* was besieged by the same. Yet here we are informed (at least we learn so from History) that it was

* See *Fabric. Bibl. Græc.* T. IV. p. 371, and *Suidas*, under the word *Herodes*.

P. III. miraculoufly faved by *Minerva* and *Achilles*. The Goddefs it feems and the Hero both of them appeared, compelling the Invader to raife the fiege*.

'TWAS thus we are told, that, many years before, *Caftor* and *Pollux* had fought for the *Romans*†; and that, many centuries afterwards, *St. George*, at *Iconium*, difcomfited the *Saracens*‡—nay, fo late as in the fixteenth century, a gallant *Spaniard*, *Peter de Paz*, was feen to affift his countrymen, *fome months after his*

* See *Zofimi Hiftor.* L. V. c. 5 and 6, p. 511, &c. *Edit. Gr. Lat.* 8vo. 1679. where the whole ftory is related at length.

† See *Florus* L. I. 2. L. II. 12.—*Juftin.* Lib. XX. 3.

‡ *Fuller's Holy War*, p. 27. *Matt. Paris*, p. 43. According to this laft Author there were three that fought, *St. George*, *St. Demetrius*, and *St. Mercury*.

deceafe,

deceaſe, when they made an aſſault at the ſiege of *Antwerp* *. Ch. III.

INSTEAD of giving my own Sentiments upon theſe events, I chuſe to give thoſe

* The following Extract is taken from the *Diſquiſitiones Magicæ* of *Martin Del-Rio*, printed at *Mentz*, an. 1617. *cum gratia et privilegio Cæſar. Majeſt.* together with the approbation of *Oliverius Manarcus*, *Vice-Provincial of the Belgic Jeſuits*, and *Gulielmus Fabricius*, ſtiled *Apoſtolicus et Regius Librorum Cenſor*; and atteſted alſo by the evidence *multorum gravium militum*, QUI VIDISSE SE SANCTE JURABANT.

The beſieged it ſeems and their Allies, *the Dutch* and *Engliſh*, were upon the point of forcing a Poſt (Aggerem) poſſeſt by the *Spaniards*, who beſieged the City.—*Del-Rio*'s words after this are—*Tum a regiis militibus* (Hiſpanis ſcil.) *primo paucioribus* CONSPECTUS PROPE AGGEREM PETRUS DE PAZ, *Hiſpanus Tribunus, vir et militarib. et pietatis ornamentis laudatiſſimus, qui, jam* MENSIBUS ALIQUOT ANTE DEFUNCTUS, *viſus his armatus*, UT SOLEBAT, legionem præcedere, *et ſuis quondam militibus*, MANU ADVOCATIS, ſequerentur *ut ſe* IMPERARE. *Indicant primi ſecundis; ſic tertiis; ſic ſequentibus*; VIDENT OMNES IDEM, *mirantur, animiſque reſumptis* NOTUM SEQUUNTUR DUCEM, *&c.* Diſquiſit. Mag. p. 262.

P. III. of an abler man upon *a similar* ſubject. After having related ſome ſingular ſtories of equal probability, *Lord Bacon* concludes with the following obſervation—

My Judgment (ſays he) *is, that they* (he means the ſtories) *ought all to be deſpiſed, and ought to ſerve but for winter-talk by the fire-ſide. Tho' when I ſay* deſpiſed, *I mean it as for Belief; for otherwiſe the ſpreading or publiſhing of them is in no ſort to be* deſpiſed, *for they have done much miſchief.*

Synesius, who lived in the fifth Century, viſited *Athens*; and gives in his Epiſtles an account of his viſit. Its luſtre appears at that time to have been greatly diminiſhed. Among other things he informs us, that the celebrated Portico or Colonade, the *Greek* name of which gave

* *Eſſays* and Counſels by *Ld. Verulam*, No. XXXV.

name to the Sect of Stoics, had by an oppressive Proconsul been despoiled of its fine Pictures; and that, on this devastation, it had been forsaken by those Philosophers *. Ch. III.

In the thirteenth Century, when the *Grecian Empire* was cruelly oppressed by the *Crusaders*, and all things in confusion, *Athens* was besieged by one *Scgurus Leo*, who was unable to take it; and, after that, by a *Marquis of Montserrat*, to whom it surrendered †.

Its fortune after this was various; and it was sometimes under the *Venetians*, sometimes under the *Catalonians*, till *Ma-*

* See *Synesii Epist.* 135. in *Gronovius's Collection*, T. V. (as before) p. 1751, and of this work, p. 265.

† See *Gronovius's Collection* (as before) p. 1751, 1752, 1753, 1754.

homet

P. III. *homet the Great* made himſelf Maſter of *Conſtantinople*. This fatal cataſtrophe (which happened near two thouſand years after the time of *Piſiſtratus*) brought ATHENS and with it all GREECE into the hands of the *Turks*, under whoſe deſpotic yoke it has continued ever ſince.

THE City from this time has been occaſionally viſited, and Deſcriptions of it publiſhed by different Travellers. WHEELER was there along with SPON in the time of our *Charles the Second*, and both of them have publiſhed curious and valuable Narratives. Others, as well natives of this Iſland, as foreigners, have been there ſince, and ſome have given (as Monſr. *Le Roy*) ſpecious publications of what we are *to ſuppoſe* they ſaw. None however have equalled the Truth, the Accuracy, and Elegance of Mr. STUART, who, after having reſided there between three and four years, has given us ſuch Plans,

Plans, and Elevations of the *capital Buildings* now ſtanding, together with learned Comments to elucidate every part, that he ſeems, as far as was poſſible for the power of *Deſcription*, to have reſtored the City to its *antient* Splendor. Ch. III.

He has not only given us the greater Outlines and their Meaſures, but ſeparate Meaſures and Drawings of the *minuter* Decorations; ſo that a *Britiſh* Artiſt may (if he pleaſe) follow Phidias, and build in *Britain*, as *Phidias* did at Athens*.

Spon, ſpeaking of *Attica*, ſays that the Road near Athens was pleaſing, and the very Peaſants poliſhed. Speaking of the *Athenians* in general, he ſays of them— *ils ont une politeſſe d'eſprit naturelle, &*

* This moſt curious and valuable Book was publiſhed at London, in the year 1762.

beau-

P. III. *beaucoup d'addresse dans toutes les affaires, qu'ils entreprenent**.

WHEELER, who was *Spon*'s fellow-traveller, says as follows, when he and his Company approached ATHENS—*We began now to think ourselves in a* MORE CIVILIZED COUNTRY, *than we had yet past: for not a Shepherd, that we met, but bid us* WELCOME, AND WISHED US *a good journey*—p. 335, speaking of the ATHENIANS, he adds—*This must with great truth be said of them, their bad fortune hath not been able to take from them, what* THEY HAVE BY NATURE, *that is, much* SUBTLETY *or* WIT. p. 347. And again—THE ATHENIANS, *notwithstanding the long possession that Barbarism hath had of this place, seem to be much* MORE POLISHED *in point of* MANNERS *and* CON-

* *Spon*, V. II. p. 76, 92, *Edit.* 8vo.

VERSATION,

VERSATION, *than any other in these parts;* *being civil, and of respectful behaviour to all, and highly complimental in their discourse* *.

STUART says of the *present Athenians,* what *Spon* and *Wheeler* said of their forefathers;—he found in them the same address, the same natural acuteness, tho' severely curbed by their despotic Masters.

ONE custom I cannot omit. He tells me, that frequently at their convivial Meetings, one of the company takes, what they now call, a Lyre, tho' it is rather a species of Guitar, and after a short prelude on the Instrument, as if he were waiting for inspiration, accompanies his instrumental Music with his voice, suddenly chanting some *extempore* Verses, which seldom exceed two or three Distichs; that he then delivers the Lyre to his neigh-

* *Wheeler*, p. 356, *Edit. Fol.*

P. III. neighbour, who, after he has done the same, delivers it to another; and that so the Lyre circulates, till it has past round the table.

Nor can I forget his informing me, that, notwithstanding *the various Fortune* of Athens, as a *City*, Attica was still famous for Olives, and Mount Hymettus for Honey. *Human Institutions perish, but Nature is permanent.*

CHAP. IV.

Account of Byzantine Scholars continued—SUIDAS—JOHN STOBÆUS *or of* STOBA—PHOTIUS—MICHAEL PSELLUS—*this last said to have commented twenty-four Plays of* MENANDER—*Reasons, to make this probable*—EUSTATHIUS, *a Bishop, the Commentator of* HOMER—EUSTRATIUS, *a Bishop, the Commentator of* ARISTOTLE—PLANUDES, *a Monk, the admirer and translator of* LATIN *Classics, as well as the Compiler of one of the present* GREEK ANTHOLOGIES.—*Conjectures concerning the duration of* THE LATIN TONGUE *at Constantinople.*

THAT I may not be prolix, I haſten from the writers already mentioned to SUIDAS, who is ſuppoſed to have lived during the ninth or tenth Centuries. In his *Lexicon,* which is partly *Hiſtorical,* partly

Ch. IV.

P. III. partly *Explanatory*, he has preserved many Quotations from Authors who lived in the earlier and politer ages, and from Poets in particular, whose works at present are for the greater part lost. KUSTER, an able Critic in the beginning of the present Century, gave a fine Edition of this Author, at *Cambridge*, in three Volumes Folio; and Mr. TOUPE *of Cornwall* (whom I have mentioned already, and cannot mention with too much applause) has lately favoured the learned world with many valuable Emendations *.

JOHN STOBÆUS or of *Stoba*, (whose name *John* makes it probable he was a *Christian)* is of an uncertain age, as well as *Suidas*; tho' some imagine him to have lived during *an earlier* period, by two or three Centuries †. His work is *not a*

---

* Concerning this little known Author see the Preface of his learned Editor, *Kuster*.

† See *Fabric. Biblioth. Græc.* T. VIII. 665.

Lexicon,

Lexicon, like that of the other, but *an immense Common-Place*, filled with Extracts upon various subjects, both *Ethical* and *Physical*, which Extracts he had collected from the most approved Writers. As this Book is highly valuable from containing such incredible variety of Sentiments upon *interesting* Topics, and those taken from Authors, many of whom are lost; as it is at the same time so incorrectly printed, that in too many places it is *hardly intelligible*: it would be a labour well worthy of an able Critic, by the help of *Manuscripts*, and plausible *Conjecture*, to restore it, as far as possible, to its original Purity. The Speculations he chiefly gives us are neither trivial, nor licentious, but, in the language of *Horace*,

Ch. IV.

— *quod magis ad nos*
Pertinet, et nescire malum est.—

But to return from Stobæus to Suidas. If we consider the late age when

P. III. *Suidas* lived; if we consider too the Authors, which he must needs have studied, in order to form his work; Authors, who many of them wrote in the most *refined* and *polished* Ages: it will be evident, that even in those *late* Centuries the Taste for *a purer Literature was by no means extinct*, and that even *then* there were Readers, who knew its value.

In the *ninth Century* lived Photius, *Patriarch of Constantinople.* His most celebrated work may be called *a Journal of his Studies*; a Journal, where we learn the various *Authors* he perused; the *Subjects* they treated; the *Plans* of their Works; and where sometimes also we have *Extracts.* From him we are informed not only of many Authors now lost, but what was in his time the state of many, that are now remaining.

Among the Authors now lost he perused Theopompus *the Historian*, and Hy-

PERIDES

PERIDES *the Orator*; among those, now mutilated and imperfect, he perused intire DIODORUS SICULUS. Many others, if necessary, might be added of either sort. Ch.IV.

'TIS singular with regard to PHOTIUS, that from a *Layman* he was raised at once to be *Patriarch of Constantinople.* Yet his Studies evidently seem to have had such a rank in view, being principally applied to *Theology*, to *History*, and to *Oratory*; with *enough Philosophy*, and *Medicine*, not to appear deficient, if such subjects should occur. As to *Poetry*, one might imagine, either that he had no relish for it, or that, in the train of his inquiries, he did not esteem it a requisite*.

MICHAEL PSELLUS, of the *eleventh Century*, was knowing in the *Greek Phi-*

---

* See *Fabric. Bibl. Græc.* T. IX. 369.

P. III. *losophy and Poetry* of the *purer* ages, and for his various and extensive Learning was ranked among the first and ablest Scholars of his time.

Besides his Treatise of *Mathematics*, his Comments upon *Aristotle*, and a number of other Works (many of which are printed) he is said to have commented and explained no less than *twenty-four Comedies* of Menander, a Treatise now lost, tho' extant as well as the Comedies in so *late* a period. He must have had a relish for that polite Writer, or otherwise 'tis not probable, he would have undertaken such a labour*.

Nor

* See *Fabric. Bibl. Græc.* T. I. 769.

In the passage, quoted by *Fabricius* upon this subject, its Author says, that the latter *Greek* Monks persuaded the latter *Greek* Emperors, to destroy *Menander* and many other of the *old Greek Poets*, from the loose-ness

Ch.IV.

Nor need we wonder this ſhould happen. Why ſhould not the polite Menander have had his Admirers in theſe Ages, as well as the licentious Aristophanes?—Or rather, why not as well as Sophocles, and Euripides? The *Scholia* upon theſe (tho' ſome perhaps may be more antient) were compiled by Critics, who lived long after Psellus*.

We may add with regard to *all theſe Scholiaſts* (whatever may have been their

---

neſs of their Morals, and their great Indecencies. That the Monks may have perſuaded this, is not improbable—perhaps from Bigotry; perhaps from a conſciouſneſs of their own wretched Inferiority in every ſpecies of elegant Compoſition—but certainly from no indignation againſt Indecency and Immorality. For if ſo, why preſerve *Lucian?* why preſerve *Ariſtophanes?* why preſerve Collections of Epigrams, more indecent and flagitious, than the groſſeſt Productions of the moſt licentious modern Ages?

* *Demetrius Triclinius*, the Scholiaſt on *Sophocles*, lived after *Planudes*, for he mentions him. See *Fabric. Bib. Græc.* p. 634.

 Age)

P. III. Age) they would never have undergone the *labours* of Compilation and Annotation, had they not been encouraged by the taste of their *Contemporary* Countrymen. For who ever published, without hopes of having Readers?

THE same may be asserted of the learned *Bishop of Thessalonica*, EUSTATHIUS, who lived in the *twelfth* Century. His admiration of HOMER must have been *almost* enthusiastic, to carry him thro' so complete, so minute, and so vast a Commentary, both upon *the Iliad* and *the Odyssey*, collected from such an immense number both of Critics and Historians*.

EUSTRATIUS, *the Metropolitan of Nice*, who lived a *little* earlier in the same Century, convinces us that he studied ARISTOTLE with no less zeal; and that, not

* See *Fabric. Biblioth. Græc.* T. I. p. 289, &c.

only

only in his *Logical* pieces, but in his *Ethical* also, as may be seen by those minute and accurate Comments on the NICOMACHEAN ETHICS, which go under his name, and in which, tho' *others* had their share, he still is found to have taken so large a Portion to himself *. Ch.IV.

PLANUDES, a Monk of the *fourteenth* Century, appears (which is somewhat uncommon) to have understood and admired THE LATIN CLASSICS, *Cicero*, *Cæsar*, *Ovid*, *Boethius*, and others, parts of which Authors he translated, such as the Commentaries of *Cæsar*, relative to the *Gallic* Wars, the Dream of Scipio by *Cicero*, the Metamorphosis of *Ovid*, the fine Tract of *Boethius de Consolatione*, and (according to Spon) *St. Augustine de Civitate Dei*. Besides this, he formed a GREEK ANTHO-

* See *Fabric. Biblioth. Græc.* T. II. p. 151.

P. III. LOGY (that well known Collection printed by *Wechelius*, in 1600,) and composed several *original* Pieces of his own *.

IT appears from *these* Examples, and will hereafter appear from *others*, how much the Cause of *Letters* and *Humanity* is indebted to THE CHURCH.

HAVING mentioned *Latin Classics*, I beg leave to submit a conjecture concerning the state and duration of the LATIN TONGUE at *Constantinople*.

WHEN CONSTANTINE founded this *Imperial City*, he not only adorned it with curiosities from every part of the *Roman Empire*, but he induced, by every sort of encouragement, many of the First Families in *Italy*, and a multitude more of in-

* See *Fabric. Biblioth. Græc:* T. X. p. 533.

ferior

ferior rank, to leave their Country, and there settle themselves. We may therefore suppose, that LATIN was for a long time the *prevailing Language* of the Place, till in a course of years it was supplanted by GREEK, the *common* Language of the neighbourhood, and the *fashionable acquired* Language of every polite *Roman*.

WE are told, that soon after the End of the *sixth* Century LATIN ceased to be spoken at ROME *. Yet was it in the beginning of that Century that JUSTINIAN published his *Laws* in LATIN at *Constantinople*; and that the celebrated PRISCIAN in the same City taught *the Principles of the Latin Grammar*.

IF we descend to a period still later, (so late indeed as to the *tenth* and *eleventh* Centuries) we shall find, in the Ceremonial of the *Byzantine* Court, certain For-

* See before, p. 238.

mularies

P. III. mularies preserved, evidently connected with this subject.

As often as the Emperor gave an Imperial Banquet, 'twas the Custom for some of his Attendants, at peculiar times during the Feast, to repeat and chant the following Words — *Κωνσέρβετ Δέους ἡμπέριουμ βέστρουμ—βήβητε, Δόμηνι ἡμπεράτωρες ἐν μούλτος ἄννος· Δέους ὀμνήποτενς πρέσεθ—Ἠν γαυδίῳ πρανδεῖτε, Δόμηνι.*

It may possibly for a moment surprise a learned Reader, when he hears that the meaning of this strange Jargon is—*May God preserve your Empire—Live, imperial Lords, for many years; God almighty so grant—Dine, my Lords, in joy.*

But his doubts will soon vanish, when he finds this Jargon to be Latin, and comes to read it exhibited according to a Latin Alphabet—

CON-

CONSERVET DEVS IMPERIVM VESTRVM—VIVITE, DOMINI IMPERATORES, IN MVLTOS ANNOS; DEVS OMNIPOTENS PRAESTET—IN GAVDIO PRANDETE, DOMINI *. Ch.IV.

'Tis evident from theſe inſtances, that traces of LATIN were ſtill remaining at *Conſtantinople*, during thoſe Centuries. 'Twill be then perhaps leſs wonderful, if PLANUDES upon the ſame ſpot ſhould, in the *fourteenth* Century, appear to have

* Theſe Formularies are ſelected from a Ceremonial of the *Byzantine* Court, drawn up by the Emperor *Conſtantine Porphyrogenitus*, who reigned in the beginning of the eleventh Century. The Book, being a large Folio, was publiſhed in the original *Greek*, with a *Latin* Tranſlation and Notes, by *Leichius* and *Reiſkius*, at *Lipſic*, in the year 1751. See of this Book p. 215, 216. Many more Traces of this *Helleniſtic Latin* occur in other parts of it. In the *Latin Types* I have followed the *Commentator*, and not *the Tranſlator*; and as the *Greeks* have no Letter but B to denote the *Latin* V, have preferred *Vivite* to *Bibite*.

under-

P. III. underſtood it. We may ſuppoſe, that by degrees it changed from a *Common* Language to a *Learned* one, and that, being thus confined to *the Learned Few*, its valuable Works were by *their* labours *again* made known, and diffuſed among their Countrymen in *Greek Tranſlations*.

THIS too will make it probable, that even to the *loweſt* age of the *Greek Empire* their great LIBRARIES contained many valuable LATIN MANUSCRIPTS; perhaps had *entire* Copies of *Cicero*, of *Livy*, of *Tacitus*, and many others. Where elſe did PLANUDES, when he tranſlated, find his *Originals*?

CHAP.

CHAP. V.

NICETAS, THE CHONIATE—*his curious Narrative of the Mischiefs done by* BALDWYN'S CRUSADE, *when they sackt* CONSTANTINOPLE *in the Year* 1205—*many of the Statues described, which they then destroyed—a fine Taste for Arts among the* GREEKS, *even in those Days, proved from this Narrative—not so, among the* CRUSADERS—*Authenticity of Nicetas's Narrative—State of* CONSTANTINOPLE *at the last Period of the Grecian Empire, as given by contemporary Writers,* PHILELPHUS *and* ÆNEAS SYLVIUS—NATIONAL PRIDE *among the Greeks not totally extinct even at this Day.*

BESIDES PLANUDES a large number of the same nation might be mentioned, but I omit them all for the sake of NICETAS, THE CHONIATE, in order to

Ch. V.

P. III. to prove thro' him, that the more refined part of that ingenious people had not even in the *thirteenth* Century *lost their Taste*; a Taste not confined to *Literary* Works only, but extended to Works of *other* kinds and character.

THIS Historian (I mean NICETAS *) was present at the sacking of *Constantinople* by the Barbarians of *Baldwyn's Crusade*, in the year 1205. Take, by the way of Sample, a part only of his Enumeration of the noble Statues, which were probably brought thither by *Constantine*, to decorate his new City, and which these *Adventurers* then destroyed †.

AMONG

* He was called the *Choniate* from *Chonæ*, a City of *Phrygia*, and possest, when in the Court of *Constantinople*, some of the highest Dignities. *Fabric. Biblioth. Græc.* T. XI. p. 401, 402.

† A large part of this Chapter is extracted from the History of *Nicetas*, as printed by *Fabricius* in the Tome above

AMONG others he mentions the *Colossian Statue* of JUNO, erected in the *Forum* of *Constantine*; the Statue of PARIS standing by VENUS, and delivering to her the Golden Apple; a square and lofty OBELISK, with a FIGURE on it to indicate the Wind; the Figure of BELLEROPHON, riding upon PEGASUS; the PENSIVE HERCULES, made by no less an Artist than LYSIPPUS; the two celebrated *Figures* of THE MAN and THE ASS, erected by *Augustus* after his Victory at *Actium*; the WOLF, suckling ROMULUS and REMUS; an EAGLE *destroying* a SERPENT, set up by *Apollonius Tyaneus*; and an *exquisite*

above quoted, beginning from p. 405, and proceeding to p 418.

The Author has endeavoured to make his translated Extracts faithful, but he thought the whole *Original Greek* too much to be inserted, especially as it may be found in *Fabricius's Bibliotheca*, a Book by no means rare. A few particular passages he has given in the *Original*.

HELEN,

P. III. HELEN, in all the Charms of Beauty and of Elegance.

SPEAKING of *the Wind-obeliſk*, he relates with the greateſt feeling the curious work on its ſides; the rural Scene; *Birds* ſinging; *Ruſtics* labouring, or playing on their Pipes; Sheep bleating; *Lambs* ſkipping; *the Sea*, and a Scene of *Fiſh* and *Fiſhing*; little naked *Cupids*, laughing, playing, and pelting each other with Apples; A FIGURE on the ſummit, turning with the ſlighteſt blaſt, and thence denominated *the Wind's Attendant.*

OF the *two Statues* brought from *Actium* he relates, that they were ſet up there by *Auguſtus* on the following Incident. As he went out by night to reconnoitre the Camp of *Antony*, he met *a Man*, driving an Aſs. The Man was aſked, *who he was*, and *whither he was going* — *my Name*, replied he, *is* NICO,

my

my Aſs's name NICANDER; *and I am going to* CÆSAR'*s Army*. The Story derives its force from the *good Omen of lucky names*, and may be found (tho' with ſome variation) both in *Suetonius* and *Plutarch*. The *real* Curioſity was, that Statues ſo celebrated ſhould be *then* exiſting. Ch. V.

IF the Figures of *the Wolf* and *the Founders of Rome* were of the ſame age, they might probably have been the very *Work*, to which VIRGIL is ſuppoſed to have alluded, in deſcribing the Shield of ENEAS:

——illam tereti cervice reflexam
Mulcere alternos, et corpora fingere lingua.
Æn. VIII. 633.

BUT no where does the Taſte of NICETAS appear ſo ſtrongly, as when he ſpeaks of the HERCULES, and the HELEN.

P. III. THE HERCULES is exhibited to us, as if he were actually present—*immense in bulk*, and, with an Air of Grandeur, *reposing* himself—his *Lion's-skin* (that lookt formidable even in brass) *thrown over him*—himself sitting without a Quiver, a Bow, or a Club, but having *the right leg bent* at the knee; *his Head* gently *reclining* on the *hand of his left Arm*; and a *Countenance full of dejection*, as if he were reflecting with indignation on the many successive labours, imposed on him by *Eurystheus**.

FOR his *Person*, we are informed he was *ample* in the *Chest*; *broad* in the *Shoulders*; had *Hair that curled*; *Arms* that were *strong* and *muscular*; and a *Mag-*

* Ἐκάθητο δὲ, μὴ γωρυτὸν ἐξημμένος, μὴ τόξον ταῖν χεροῖν φέρων, μὴ, κ. τ. λ. *Fabr.* as above, p. 408, 409.

nitude

nitude ſuch, as might be ſuppoſed to belong to the ORIGINAL HERCULES, were he to revive; *a Leg* being equal in length to the Stature of a *common* Man*. And yet adds NICETAS, filled with Indignation, "this Hercules, being ſuch as here re-"preſented, this very Hercules did not "theſe men ſpare." Ch. V.

I can only ſubjoin, by way of digreſſion, that there is a fine *Greek* Epigram deſcribing the Statue of a DEJECTED HERCULES, ſitting without his Weapons, which exactly reſembles this of Nicetas, and which is ſaid likewiſe to be the work of LYSIPPUS, only there the Poet imputes his Hero's *Dejection*, not to the Tyranny of *Euryſtheus*, but to the love of *Omphale* †.

* Ἦν δὲ τὸ ϛέρνον εὐρὺς, τὰς ὤμους πλατὺς, τὴν τρίχα ὅλος, κ. τ. λ. Ibid. p. 409.

† Vid. *Antholog.* L. IV. tit. 8.

P. III. If *Nicetas* ſpeak with *admiration* of *this* Statue, 'tis with *rapture* he mentions *the other*. "*What*, ſays he, *ſhall I ſay of* "*the beauteous* HELEN; *of her, who* "*brought together all Greece againſt Troy?* "*Did ſhe* MITIGATE *theſe* IMMITI- "GABLE, *theſe* IRON-HEARTED *Men?* "*No*," ſays he, "*nothing like it could* "*even ſhe affect, who had before enſlaved* "*ſo many Spectators with her Beauty**."

AFTER this he deſcribes her Dreſs, and then proceeds to her *Perſon*; which Deſcription, as it is ſomething ſingular, I have endeavoured to tranſlate more ſtrictly.

"HER LIPS" (ſays he) "*like opening* "*Flowers, were gently parted, as if ſhe*

* Ἆρ' ἐμείλιξε τοὺς δυσμειλίκτους; ἆρ', ἐμάλθαξε τοὺς σιδηρόφρονας; οὐ μὴν οὖν οὐδὲ ὅλως τοιοῦτον τι δεδύνηται ἡ πάντα θεατὴν τῷ κάλλει δουλαγωγήσασα, καίπερ, κ. τ. λ. *Fabric.* ut ſupra, p. 412. 413.

"*was*

" *was going to speak: and as for that* " GRACEFUL SMILE, *which instantly met* " *the beholder, and filled him with delight;* " *those elegant* CURVATURES OF HER " EYE-BROWS, *and the remaining* HARMONY OF HER FIGURE; *they were what* " *no Words can describe, and deliver down* " *to Posterity**."

HE then breaks into an Exclamation— " *But O!* HELEN, *Thou pure and genuine* " *Beauty; Offspring of the Loves; decorated by the Care of* VENUS; *most exquisite of Nature's Gifts; Prize of Contest between Trojans and Grecians:* " *where was thy* NEPENTHES, *that* " *soothing Draught, which thou learnedst* " *in Egypt?—Where thy irresistible Love-* " *charms?—Why didst Thou uot employ*

---

* Ἦν δὲ κ̀ τὰ χείλη, καλύκων δίκην, ἠρέμα παρανοιγόμενα, ὡς κ̀ δοκεῖν, κ. τ. λ. Ibid. p. 413.

P. III.

"them now, as thou didst in days of yore?
"Alas! I fear 'twas destined by Fate,
"that Thou shouldst perish by Flames;
"Thou, who didst not cease even in thy
"Statue to inflame beholders into Love.
"I could almost say that these SONS OF
"ENEAS had demolished Thee by FIRE,
"as a species of retaliation for the BURN-
"ING OF THEIR TROY, as those Flames
"were kindled by thy unfortunate A-
"mours*."

I have been thus particular in these Relations, and have translated for the greater part the very *words* of the Historian, not only because the Facts are little known, but because they tend to prove, that even in those *dark* Ages (as we have too many

* Ἀλλ᾽ Ὦ Τυνδαρὶς Ἑλένη, κάλλος αὐτόθεν καλὸν, Ἐρώτων μόσχευμα, Ἀφροδίτης τημελέχημα, πανάριστον φύσεως δώρημα, Τρώων καὶ Ἑλλήνων βράβευμα, ποῦ σοι τὸ Νηπενθὲς, κ. τ. λ. Ibid. p. 413.

reasons

reaſons to call them) there were *Greeks ſtill extant*, who had *a Taſte for the finer Arts*, and an *Enthuſiaſtic Feeling* of their exquiſite *Beauty*. At the ſame time we cannot without indignation reflect on theſe *brutal Cruſaders*, who, after many inſtances of *ſacrilegious* Avarice, related by *Nicetas* in conſequence of their Succeſs, could deſtroy all *theſe*, and many other precious *Remains of Antiquity, melting them down (for they were of Braſs) into Money to pay their Soldiers, and exchanging things of ineſtimable Value for a poor pittance of contemptible Coin**. They ſurely were what NICETAS well calls them, Τȣ͂ καλȣ͂ ἀνέραςοι βάρβαροι, BARBARIANS *devoid of taſte for the* BEAUTIFUL *and* FAIR†.

Ch. V.

---

* Κεκόφασιν [ἀγάλματα] εἰς νομίσμα, ἀνταλασσόμενοι μικρῶν τὰ μεγάλα, καὶ τὰ δαπάναις πονηθέντα μεγίςαις ȣ̓τιδανῶν ἀντιδιδόντες κερμάτων. Ibid. p. 408.

† I have given the words of *Nicetas* himſelf, which precede the paſſage juſt quoted. In another part

P. III. AND yet 'tis remarkable, that these *sad* and *savage* Events happened *more than a Century after* these Adventurers had first past into the East, above *four-score years of which* time they had possessed *the Sovereignty* of *Palestine.* But—

COELUM, *non* ANIMUM *mutant*, &c.
HOR.*

THO' I have done with these Events, I cannot quit THE GREEKS without adding a

---

of his Narrative he stiles them ILLITERATE BARBARIANS; *who absolutely did not know their A B C.*— παρ' ἀγραμμάτοις βαρβάροις, καὶ τέλεον ἀναλφαβήτοις — p. 414.

* It ought to be observed, that tho' the NARRATIVE of *Nicetas*, whence these Extracts are taken, appear not in the printed Editions (being probably either thro' fraud, or shame, or both, designedly omitted,) yet has it been published by that *honest* and *learned Critic* FABRICIUS, in the *sixth* Volume of his *Bibliotheca Græca* here quoted, and is still extant in a *fair* and *antient Manuscript* of the two last Books of *Nicetas*, preserved in THE BODLEIAN LIBRARY.

word

word upon CONSTANTINOPLE, as to *Literature* and *Language*, just *before* the fatal period, when it was taken by the TURKS. There is more stress to be laid upon my Quotations, as they are transcribed from Authors, who lived at *the time*, or immediately after. Ch. V.

HEAR what PHILELPHUS says, who was himself at *Constantinople* in that part of the fifteenth Century, while the *Greek* Empire *still* subsisted. "*Those* GREEKS "(says he) *whose Language has not been* "*depraved, and whom we ourselves both* "*follow and imitate, speak even at this* "*time in their ordinary talk, as the Comic* "ARISTOPHANES *did, or the Tragic* EURIPIDES; *as the Orators would talk; as* "*the Historians; as the Philosophers them-* "*selves, even* PLATO *and* ARISTOTLE *."

SPEAK-

* *Græci, quibus lingua depravata non sit, et quos ipsi tùm sequimur, tùm imitamur, ita loquuntur vulgo hâc etiam*

P. III.

SPEAKING afterwards of the *Corruption* of the Tongue in that City by the Concourse of Traders, and Strangers, he informs us, that the People belonging *to the Court* still retained "*the* ANTIENT "*Dignity and Elegance of Speech, and* "*above all* THE WOMEN OF QUALITY, "*who, as they were wholly precluded from* "*Strangers,* STILL PRESERVED *that ge-* "*nuine and pure Speech of the* ANTIENT "GREEKS, *uncorrupted* *.

ÆNEAS

etiam in tempestate, ut Aristophanes Comicus, ut Euripides Tragicus, ut Oratores omnes, ut Philosophi etiam ipsi et Plato et Aristoteles. Philelph. Epist. in Hodii de Græcis illustribus Lib. I. p. 188.

* The same *Philelphus* in the same Epistle adds—*Nam* VIRI AULICI *veterem sermonis dignitatem atque elegantiam retinebant; in primisque* IPSÆ NOBILES MULIERES, quibus cum *nullum esset omnino cum viris peregrinis Commercium,* MERUS ILLE AC PURUS GRÆCORUM SERMO SERVABATUR INTACTUS. *Hod ut supra.*

'Tis somewhat singular, that what *Philelphus* relates concerning *the Women of Rank at the Court of Constantinople,*

ÆNEAS SYLVIUS, afterwards Pope by the name of PIUS THE SECOND, was the Scholar of this *Philelphus*. A long Letter of his is extant upon the taking of *Constantinople by Mahomet*, a Letter addreſt to a Cardinal, juſt after that fatal Event. Speaking of the fortune of the City, he obſerves, that NEW ROME (for ſo they often called CONSTANTINOPLE) had ſub- Ch. V.

tinople, ſhould be related by *Cicero* concerning *the Women of Rank* in the poliſhed days of the *Roman Commonwealth*; concerning *Cornelia*, Mother of the *Gracchi*; concerning *Lælia*, Daughter of the great *Lælius*; concerning the *Muciæ*, the *Liciniæ*, in ſhort, the Mothers, Wives, and Daughters of the moſt illuſtrious *Romans* of that illuſtrious age.

Cicero accounts for *the purity of their Language*, and for its being untainted with *vitious novelty*, preciſely as *Philelphus* does.—*Facilius enim* MULIERES INCORRUPTAM ANTIQUITATEM CONSERVANT, *quod*, MULTORUM SERMONIS EXPERTES, *ea tenent ſemper, quæ prima didicerunt.*

This Paſſage is no ſmall ſtrengthening of *Philelphus*'s Authority. See *Cicer. de Oratore* III. 45. & *de Claris Orator.* ſ. 211.

ſiſted

P. III. fiſted, from its foundation to its capture, nearly the *ſame* number of years with OLD ROME—that between ROMULUS, the founder of *Old Rome*, and the Goth, ALARIC, who took it, was an interval of about *eleven hundred years*; and that there was nearly the ſame interval between CONSTANTINE and MAHOMET THE GREAT.

HE obſerves that tho' this *laſt City* had been taken before, it had never before ſuffered ſo *total* and ſo *fatal* a change. "*Till this period* (ſays he) *the remembrance* "*of* ANTIENT WISDOM *remained at* CON- "STANTINOPLE; *and, as if it were the* "*Manſion the Seat of Letters, no one of* "*the Latins could be deemed ſufficiently* "*learned, if he had not ſtudied for ſome* "*time at* CONSTANTINOPLE. *The ſame* "*Reputation for Sciences, which* ATHENS "*had in the times of antient* Rome, *did* "CONSTANTINOPLE *appear to poſſeſs in*

"*our*

"*our times. 'Twas thence, that* PLATO Ch. V.
"*was restored to us; 'twas thence, that*
"*the Works of* ARISTOTLE, DEMOS-
"THENES, XENOPHON, THUCYDIDES,
"BASIL, DIONYSIUS, ORIGEN *and others*
"*were, in our days, made known; and*
"*many more in futurity we hoped would*
"*become so. But now, as the Turks have*
"*conquered*, &c.*"

A little farther in the same Epistle, when he expresses his fears, lest THE TURKS

---

* —*itaque mansit in hunc diem vetustæ sapientiæ apud* CONSTANTINOPOLIM *monumentum: ac, velut ibi domicilium Literarum esset, et arx summæ philosophiæ, nemo Latinorum satis doctus videri poterat, nisi Constantinopoli aliquandem studuisset; quodque florente Româ doctrinarum nomen habuerunt Athenæ, id tempestate nostra videbatur Constantinopolis obtinere. Inde nobis Plato redditus: inde Aristotelis, Demosthenis, Xenophontis, Thucididis, Basilii, Dionysii, Origenis et aliorum multa Latinis opera diebus nostris manifestata sunt; multa quoque in futurum manifestanda sperabamus. Nunc vero, vincentibus Turcis,* &c. Æneæ Sylv. Epist. p. 704. 705. *Edit. Basil.* 1551.

should

P. III. ſhould deſtroy all Books but their own, he ſubjoins—"*Now therefore both* HOMER, "*and* PINDAR, *and* MENANDER, *and all* "*the more illuſtrious Poets will undergo a* "*ſecond Death. Now will a final de*- "*ſtruction find its way to the* GREEK "PHILOSOPHERS. *A little light will* "*remain perhaps among the* LATINS, "*but that I apprehend will not be long,* "*unleſs* GOD *from Heaven will look upon* "*us with a more favourable eye, and grant* "*a better fortune either to the Roman Em*- "*pire, or to the Apoſtolic See*, &c. &c. *"

* *Nunc ergo et Homero, et Pindaro, Menandro, et omnibus illuſtrioribus Poetis ſecunda mors erit; nunc Græcorum philoſophorum ultima patebit interitus. Reſtabit aliquid lucis apud Latinos; at, fateor, neque id erit diuturnum, niſi mitiori nos oculo Deus ex alto reſpexerit, fortunamque vel imperio Romano, vel Apoſtolicæ ſedi præbuerit meliorem*, &c. &c. Ibid. p. 705, 706.

Thoſe who have not the old Edition of *Æneas Sylvius*, may find the above quotations in *Hody de Græcis Illuſtribus*, Lond. 1751. 8vo.

IT

IT muſt be remarked that, in this Epiſtle, by LATINS* he means *the Weſtern Europeans*, as oppoſed to THE GREEKS, or *Eaſtern*; and that by the ROMAN Empire (juſt before mentioned) he means the GERMANIC Body.

THE Author's apprehenſions for the fate of Letters *in the Weſt* was premature; for, upon the Deſtruction of this *imperial* City, the number of *learned Greeks*, which this Event drove into thoſe Weſtern parts of *Europe*; the Favour of the *Popes* and the *Medici* Family, ſhewn at this period to Literature; together with the then recent *Invention of Printing*, which, by multiplying Copies of Books, made them ſo eaſy to be purchaſed—all this (I ſay) tended to promote the Cauſe *of Knowlege* and *of Taſte*, and to put things into that

* *Nicetas* had before called them, SONS OF ÆNEAS. See p. 310.

train,

 train, in which we hope they may long continue.

BESIDES *Philelphus*, *Æneas Sylvius*, and many others, who were *Italians*, I might mention two *Greeks of the same age*, GEORGE GEMISTUS, and Cardinal BESSARIO, both of them deeply knowing in *Grecian Literature* and *Philosophy*.

BUT as some account of these last and of their Writings has been already given*, I shall quit the *Greeks*, after I have related a short Narrative; a Narrative so far curious, as it helps to prove, that even among the *present Greeks*, in the day of *Servitude*, the remembrance of their *antient* Glory is *not yet* totally extinct.

WHEN the late Mr. *Anson* (Lord *Anson*'s Brother) was upon his Travels in *the East*, he hired a Vessel, to visit the

* See *Philosoph. Arrangements*, p. 238, 239.

Isle of *Tenedos*. His Pilot, *an old Greek*, as they were sailing along, said with some satisfaction, — *There 'twas our Fleet lay*. Mr. *Anson* demanded, *What Fleet?*— *What Fleet*, replied the old Man (a little piqued at the Question)—WHY OUR GRECIAN FLEET AT THE SIEGE OF TROY*. Ch. V.

BUT we must now quit *the Greeks*, and, in consequence of our plan, pass to the ARABIANS, *followers of Mahomet*.

---

* This story was told *the Author* by *Mr. Anson himself*.

P. III.

CHAP. VI.

Concerning THE SECOND CLASS *of Geniuses during the middle Age*, THE ARABIANS, *or* SARACENS—*at first, barbarous—their Character before the time of Mahomet—Their greatest Caliphs were from among the* ABASSIDÆ—ALMANZUR *one of the first of that race*—ALMAMUM *of the same race, a great Patron of Learning, and learned Men*—ARABIANS *cultivated Letters, as their Empire grew settled and established—Translated the best Greek Authors into their own Language—Historians*, ABULPHARAGIUS, ABULFEDA, BOHADIN—*Extracts from the last concerning* SALADIN.

THE ARABIANS* began ill. The Sentiment of their Caliph OMAR, when

* As many Quotations are made in the following Chapters from *Arabian* Writers, and more particularly from

when he commanded the *Alexandrian Library* to be burnt (a fact we have already related*) was natural to any Bigot, when in the plentitude of Despotism. But they grew more rational, as they grew less bigotted, and by degrees began to think, that Science was worth cultivating. They may be said indeed to have recurred to their *antient* Character; that Character, which they did not rest upon brutal Force alone, but which they boasted to imply three capital things, *Hospitality*, *Valour*, and *Eloquence* †.

Ch. IV.

---

from ABULPHARAGIUS, ABULFEDA, and BOHADIN, a short account of those three authors will be given in the Notes of *this* Chapter, where their Names come in course to be mentioned.

* See before, p. 252.

† *Schultens* in his *Monumenta retustiora Arabiæ* (Lugdun. Batavor. 1740) gives us in his Preface the following Passage from *Saphadius*, an *Arabic* Author. ARABES *antiquitus non habebant, quo gloriarentur, quam* GLADIO, HOSPITE, *et* ELOQUENTIA.

P. III. WHEN Succeſs in Arms has defeated Rivals, and Empire becomes not only extended but *eſtabliſhed*, then is it that Nations begin to think of *Letters*, and to cultivate Philoſophy, and liberal Speculation. This happened to *the Athenians*, after they had triumphed over the *Perſians*; to the *Romans*, after they triumphed over *Carthage*; and to the ARABIANS, after the *Caliphate* was eſtabliſhed at *Bagdad**.

AND here perhaps it may not be improper to obſerve, that after the four firſt Caliphs, came the Race of the OMMIADÆ. Theſe about thirty years after *Mahomet*, upon the deſtruction of *Ali*, uſurped the Sovereignty, and held it ninety years. They were conſidered by the *Arabic* Hiſtorians as a race of Tyrants, and were in

* See before, p. 256, 257.

number

number fourteen*. Having made themselves by their oppressions to be much detested, the last of them, *Merwin*, was deposed by *Al-Suffah*, from whom began another race, the race of ABASSIDÆ†, who claimed to be related in blood to *Mahomet*, by descending from his Uncle, *Abbas*. Ch.VI.

As many of these were far superior in character to their predecessors, so their Dominion was of much longer duration, lasting for more than five Centuries.

THE former part of this Period may be called the Æra of *the Grandeur*, and *Magnificence* of THE CALIPHATE,

---

* See *Herbelot's Bibliotheque Orientale*, under the word OMMIADES, also *Abulpharagius*, p. 138, 160. and in particular *Abulfeda*, p. 138, &c.

† *Abulphar.* p. 138—150, &c. *Abulfeda*, p. 143. *Herbelot's Bib. Orient.* under the word ABASSIDES.

P. III. ALMANZUR, who was among the first of them, removed the imperial Seat from *Damascus* to *Bagdad*, a City which he himself founded upon the banks of the *Tigris*, and which soon after became one of the most splendid Cities throughout the *East*.

Almanzur was not only a great Conqueror, but a lover of Letters and learned Men. 'Twas under him that *Arabian* Literature, which had been at first chiefly confined to Medicine and a few other branches, was extended to Sciences of every denomination *.

HIS Grandson ALMAMUN (who reigned about fifty years after) giving a full Scope to his love of Learning, sent to the *Greek* Emperors for Copies of their *best* Books;

* See *Abulfeda*, p. 144. *Abulpharag.* p. 139. 141. 160.

em-

Ch.VI.

employed the ableſt Scholars, that could be found, *to tranſlate* them; and, when tranſlated, encouraged men of genius in their peruſal, taking a pleaſure in being preſent at *literary Converſations*. Then was it that learned men, in the lofty Language of *Eaſtern* Eloquence, were called *Luminaries, that diſpel darkneſs; Lords of human kind; of whom, when the World becomes deſtitute, it becomes barbarous and ſavage* *.

The rapid Victories of theſe *Eaſtern* Conquerors ſoon carried their Empire from *Aſia* even into the remote regions of *Spain*. Letters *followed* them, as they went. *Plato*, *Ariſtotle*, and their beſt Greek Commen-

* See *Abulfeda*, p. 181. *Abulpharag.* p. 160, 161. *The lofty Language* alluded to ſtands thus in the *Latin* Verſion of the page laſt quoted. *Docti tenebrarum lumina ſunt, et generis humani domini, quibus deſtitutus ferus evadit mundus.*

P. III. tators were ſoon tranſlated into *Arabic*; ſo were *Euclid*, *Archimedes*, *Apollonius*, *Diophantus*, and the other Greek *Mathematicians*; ſo *Hippocrates*, *Galen*, and the beſt profeſſors of *Medicine*; ſo *Ptolemy*, and the noted Writers on the ſubject of *Aſtronomy*. The ſtudy of theſe Greeks produced others like them; produced others, who not only explained them in *Arabic* Comments, but compoſed *themſelves* original pieces upon the ſame Principles.

AVERROES was celebrated for his Philoſophy in *Spain*; ALPHARABI and AVICENNA were equally admired thro' *Aſia**. Science (to ſpeak a little in their own ſtile) may be ſaid to have extended

—— a Gadibus uſque
Auroram et Gangem ——

* See *Herbelot*, under the ſeveral Names here quoted.

NOR,

Ch.VI.

NOR, in this immenſe multitude, did they want *Hiſtorians*, ſome of which (ſuch as ABULFEDA, ABULPHARAGIUS, BOHADIN*, and others) have been tranſlated,

---

* ABULFEDA was an *Oriental Prince*, deſcended from the ſame Family with the great *Saladin*. He died in the year 1345, and publiſhed *a General Hiſtory*, in which however he is *moſt particular* and diffuſe in the Narrative of *Mahomet*, and his Succeſſors.

Learned Men have publiſhed different parts of this curious Author. *Gagnier* gave us in *Arabic* and *Latin* as much of him, as related to *Mahomet*. This was printed in a thin Folio at *Oxford*, in the year 1723.

The largeſt Portion, and from which moſt of the facts here related are taken, was publiſhed by *Reiſke*, or *Reiſkius* (a very able Scholar) in *Latin only*, and includes the Hiſtory of the *Arabians* and their *Caliphs*, from the firſt year of the *Mahometan Æra*, *An. Dom.* 622, to their 406th year, *An. Dom.* 1015. This Book, a moderate or thin Quarto, was printed at *Lipſic*, in the year 1754.

We have another Portion of a period *later ſtill* than this, publiſhed by *Schultens* in *Arabic* and *Latin*; a Portion relative to the Life of *Saladin*, and ſubjoined by *Schultens* to the Life of that great Prince by *Bohadin*,

P. III. lated, and are perused, even in their Translations, both with pleasure aud profit,

---

hadin, which he (Schultens) published. But more of this hereafter.

ABULPHARAGIUS gave likewise *a general History*, divided into nine *Dynasties*, but is far more minute and diffuse (as well as *Abulfeda)* in his History of *Mahomet* and *the Caliphs*.

He was a Christian, and the Son of a Christian Physician — was an *Asiatic* by birth, and wrote in *Arabic*, as did *Abulfeda*. He brought down his History a little below the time of the celebrated *Jingez Chan*, that is to the middle of the thirteenth Century, the time when he lived. A fine Edition of this Author was given in *Arabic* and *Latin*, by the learned *Pocacke*, in two small Quartos, at Oxford, 1663.

BOHADIN wrote the Life of the celebrated *Saladin*, but more particularly that part of it, which respects the *Crusades*, and *Saladin*'s taking of *Jerusalem*. *Bohadin* has many things to render his History highly valuable: he was a *Contemporary* Writer; was an *Eye-witness of almost every Transaction*; and what is more, instead of being an obscure Man, was *high in office*, a *favourite* of *Saladin's*, and *constantly about his person*. This author flourished in the twelfth Century, that is in fit, as they give not only the outlines of Ch. VI amazing Enterprifes, but a fample of Manners, and Character, widely differing from our own.

No Hiftory perhaps can be more curious than the Life of SALADIN by BOHADIN. This Author was a conftant Attendant upon the perfon of this great Prince thro' all his active and important

---

in the time of *Saladin* and King *Richard*, *Saladin's* antagonift.

BOHADIN'S Hiftory in *Arabic* and *Latin*, with much excellent Erudition, was publifhed in an elegant Folio, by that accurate Scholar, *Schultens*, at *Leyden*, in the year 1755.

It muft be obferved that, tho' ABULPHARAGIUS was a *Chriftian*, yet ABULFEDA and BOHADIN were both *Mahometans*. All three Hiftorians bear a great refemblance to *Plutarch*, as they have enriched their Hiftories with fo many ftriking *Anecdotes*. From ABULPHARAGIUS too, and ABULFEDA, we have much curious information as to the *Progrefs and State of Literature* in thofe Ages and Countries.

Life,

P. III. Life, down to his laſt Sickneſs, and the very hour of his Death. The many curious Anecdotes, which he relates, give us the ſtriking Picture of an Eaſtern Hero.

TAKE the following Inſtance of *Saladin*'s Juſtice and Affability.

"HE was in company once with his "intimate Friends, enjoying their con-"verſation apart, the crowd being diſ-"miſt, when a Slave of ſome rank brought "him a petition in behalf of a perſon "oppreſt. The Sultan ſaid, that he was "then fatigued, and wiſhed the matter, "whatever it was, might for a time be "deferred. The other did not attend to "what was deſired, but on the contrary "almoſt thruſt the petition into the Sul-"tan's face. The Sultan on this, open-"ing and reading it over, declared he "thought the Petitioners Cauſe a good

"one.

"one.—*Let then our Sovereign Lord,* ſays "the other, *ſign it.—There is no Ink-"ſtand,* ſays the Sultan (who, being at "that time ſeated at the Door of his "Tent, rendered it impoſſible for any "one to enter)—*You have one,* replies "the Petitioner, *in the inner part of your "Tent,* (which meant, as the Writer well "obſerves, little leſs than bidding the "Prince go and bring it himſelf.) The "Sultan, looking back and ſeeing the "Ink-ſtand behind him, cries out, *God "help me, the man ſays true,* and imme-"diately reached back for it, and ſigned "the Inſtrument."

Here the Hiſtorian, who was preſent, ſpoke the language of a good Courtier. "*God Almighty,* ſaid he, *bore this Teſti-"mony to our Prophet, that* HIS *Diſpoſi-"tion was a ſublime one: our Sovereign "Lord, I perceive, has a Temper like him,* "The Sultan not regarding the Compli-"ment,

P. III. "ment, replied coolly.—*The Man did no* " *harm; we have diſpatched his buſineſs,* " *and the Reward is at hand**."

After this fact we ſhall the more readily believe *Bohadin*, when ſpeaking of the ſame illuſtrious perſon, he informs us, that his Converſation was remarkably elegant and pleaſing; that he was a perfect maſter of the Arabian Families, of their Hiſtory, their Rites, and Cuſtoms; that he knew alſo the Genealogies of their Horſes (for which we know that to this hour Arabia is celebrated;) nor was he ignorant of what was rare and curious in the world at large; that he was particularly affable in his inquiries about the Health of his Friends, their Illneſs, their Medicines, &c. that his Diſcourſe was free from all obſcenity and ſcandal; and that

* See *Bohadin*, p. 22.

he

he was remarkably tender and compaſſionate both to orphans and to perſons in years*. Ch.VI.

I may add from the ſame authority an inſtance of his Juſtice.

"As BOHADIN, the Hiſtorian, was one
" day exerciſing at *Jeruſalem* his office of
" a Judge, a decent old Merchant ten-
" dered him a Bill or Libel of Complaint,
" which he inſiſted upon having opened.
" *Who* (ſays Bohadin) *is your Adverſary?*
" —*My Adverſary*, replies the Merchant,
" *is the Sultan himſelf: but this is the Seat*
" *of Juſtice, and we have heard that you*
" (applying to Bohadin) *are not governed*
" *by regard to Perſons.* *Bohadin* told him
" the Cauſe could not be decided without
" his Adverſary's being firſt apprized.

* See *Bohadin*, p. 28. and at the end of *Bohadin*, the *Excerpta* from *Abulfeda*, p. 62, 63.

P. III. "The Sultan accordingly was informed "of the affair; submitted to appear; pro-"duced his Witnesses; and, having justly "defended himself, gained the Cause. "Yet so little did he resent this Treat-"ment, that he dismist his Antagonist "with a rich Garment and a Dona-"tion*."

His *Severity* upon occasions was no less conspicuous, than his *Clemency*.

We learn from the same Writer, that *Arnold*, Lord of *Cracha*, (called *Reginald* by M. *Paris*, and *Rainold* by *Fuller*) had thought proper, during the Truce between the *Christians* and the *Saracens*, to fall upon the Caravan of Travellers going to *Mecca* from *Egypt*, whom he cruelly pillaged and thrust into Dungeons, and when they ap-

* See *Bohadin*, p. 10.

pealed

pealed to the Truce for better ufage, replied with fcorn, *Let your Mahomet deliver you.* Ch. VI.

Saladin, fired with indignation at this perfidy, vowed a Vow to difpatch him *with his own hand*, if he could ever make him prifoner. The Event happened at the fatal Battle of *Hittyn*, where *Guy* King of Jerufalem, *Arnold*, and all the principal Commanders of the *Christian* Army were taken. *Saladin*, as foon as his Tent could be erected, in the height of his Feftivity, orders King *Guy*, his Brother *Geoffry*, and Prince *Arnold* into his prefence.

As *Guy* the King was nearly dying for thirft, *Saladin* prefented him a delicious Cup, cooled with Snow, out of which the King drank, and then tranfmitted it to *Arnold*. *Tell the King*, fays the Sultan, turning to his Interpreter, *tell him*,

Z THOU,

P. III. THOU, *King*, *art* HE, *who hast given the Cup to* THIS MAN, *and not* I.

Now it is a most admirable Custom (observes *Bohadin*) among the *Arabians*, a custom breathing their liberal and noble disposition, that a Captive, the moment he has obtained meat or drink from his Captor, is by that very treatment rendered secure of Life, the *Arabians* being a people, by whom HOSPITALITY and the generous *point of honour* is most sacredly observed.

THE Prisoners, being dismist, were soon remanded, when only the Sultan and a few of his Ministers were left. *Arnold* was the first brought in, whom the Sultan reminding of his irreverent Speech, subjoined, *See* ME *now act the part of Mahomet's Avenger*. He then offers *Arnold* to embrace the *Mahometan* Faith, which he refusing, the Sultan with his

his drawn ſcymitar gave him a ſtroke, that broke the hilt, while the reſt of his attendants joined and diſpatched him. King *Guy* thought the ſame deſtiny was prepared for him. The Sultan however *bid him be of good cheer*, obſerving, that *it was not cuſtomary for Kings to kill Kings; but that this Man had brought deſtruction upon himſelf by paſſing the Bounds of all Faith and Honour* *.

Ch. VI.

WHEN Princes are victorious, their Rigour is often apt to extend too far, eſpecially where Religion, as in theſe Wars called HOLY, blends itſelf with the tranſaction.

MORE than fourſcore years before *Saladin*'s time the Cruſaders, when they

* See *Bohadin*, p. 27. 28. 70. 71.

P. III. took *Jerusalem*, had murdered every *Mahometan* they found there *.

When *Saladin* took *Jerusalem*, he had at first meditated putting all the *Franks* to the sword, as a sort of retaliation for what had been done there by these first Crusaders. However he was persuaded to change his intention, and spare them: nay more, after he had turned the rest of their Churches into Mosques, he still left them one, in which they had Toleration to perform their worship †.

After the fatal Battle of *Hittyn*, where *Guy* and *Arnold* (as above mentioned) were taken, *Saladin* divided his Prisoners;

* See *Abulpharagius*, p. 243. *Matt. Par.* in anno 1099. p. 48. *Fuller's Holy Warre*, B. I. c. 24. p. 141.

† See *Abulpharagius*, p. 273. *Bohadin*, p. 73. *Abulfedæ Exerpta*, p. 42. *Matth. Paris*, p. 145. *Fuller's H. Warre*, B. II. c. 46. p. 106.

some

ſome were ſold; others pnt to death; and among the laſt all the commanders of the *Hoſpitalers* and *Templars*. Ch. VI.

On the taking of *Ptolemais* by the Cruſaders, ſome difference ariſing between them and *Saladin* about the Terms of the Capitulation, the Cruſaders led the Captive *Muſſelmans* out of the City into a Plain, and there in cold blood murdered three thouſand *.

Cuſtoms in all times, and in all Countries, have a ſingular effect. When the French Ambaſſádors were introduced to *Saladin*, he was playing with a favourite Son, by name *Elemir*.. The Child no ſooner beheld the Embaſſadors with their Faces ſhaved, their Hair cut,

* See *Bohadin*, p. 70, for the *Templars*, and p. 183, for the *Muſulmans* — alſo *Fuller's H. Warre*, B. II. c. 45. p. 105.

P. III. and their Garments of an unuſual form, than he was terrified, and began to cry. A Beard perhaps would have terrified a Child in *France:* and yet, if Beards are the gift of Nature, it ſeems eaſier to defend the little Arabian *.

Bohadin, our Hiſtorian, appears to have thought ſo, who, mentioning a young *Frank* of high Quality, deſcribes him to be a fine Youth, except that his Face was *ſhaved*; a *Mark,* as he calls it, by which the *Franks* are diſtinguiſhed †.

We cannot quit *Saladin,* without a word on his *Liberality.*

He uſed to ſay, 'twas poſſible there might exiſt a man (and by ſuch man 'twas

* See *Bohadin,* p. 270.

† See *Bohadin,* p. 193.

ſup-

supposed he meant *himself*) who with the same eye of contempt could look on *Riches* and on *Dirt* *. Ch. VI.

These seem to have been his Sentiments, when some of his Revenue-officers were convicted of putting into his Treasury Purses of Brass for Purses of Gold. By the rigour of Eastern Justice they might have immediately been executed; but *Saladin* did no more than dismiss them from their office †.

When his Treasury was so empty, that he could not supply his Largesses, in order to have it in his power, he sold his very furniture ‡.

When his Army was encamped in the Plains of *Ptolemaïs*, 'twas computed he

---

* See *Bohadin*, p. 13.

† See *Bohadin*, p. 27.

‡ See *Bohadin*, 12, 13.

P. III. gave away no less than twelve thousand Horses; nay, 'twas said he never mounted a Horse, which was not either *given away*, or *promised**.

Bohadin, whom he employed in most of his acts of *Munificence*, relates, that all who approached him, were sensible of its effects; nay that he exceeded in his Donations even the unreasonable wishes of the Petitioners, altho' he was *never heard to boast* of any favour that he had conferred †.

The effect of such immense *Liberality* was, that, when he died, out of all the vast revenues of *Egypt*, *Syria*, the *Oriental Provinces*, and *Arabia Felix*, there was no more left in his Treasury, than forty

* See *Bohadin*, p. 13.—The same Book, in the Extract from *Abulfeda*, p. 62.

† See *Bohad.* p. 13.

seven

ſeven pieces of Silver, and one of Gold; ſo that they were forced to borrow money, to defray the expences of his Funeral *. Ch. VI.

As to the facts reſpecting the Weſtern Cruſaders at this period, and particularly *Saladin*'s great Antagoniſt, *Richard Coeur de Leon*, theſe are ſubjects reſerved, till we come to the *Latins* or *Franks*.

We ſhall now ſay ſomething concerning *Arabian* Poetry and Works of *Invention*, adding withal a few more Anecdotes, relative to their *Manners* and *Character*.

* See *Bohadin*, p 5: 13 and, in the ſame Book, the Extracts from *Abulfeda*, p 62.—*Abulpharagius*, p. 277. See *Fuller*'s Character of *Saladin*, *Holy Warre*, B. III. ch. 14. as alſo the above Extracts, and *Abulpharagius*, both under the ſame pages.

CHAP.

CHAP. VII.

Arabian Poetry, *and Works of Invention — Facts relative to their Manners and Characters.*

ARABIAN POETRY is so immense a Field, that he, who enters it, is in danger of being lost. 'Twas their favourite study long before the time of *Mahomet*, and many Poems are still extant of an earlier Æra*. So much did they value themselves upon the Elegance of their Compositions, that they called their neighbours, and more particularly the *Persians*, BARBARIANS†. It seems un-

* See *Schultens* in his *Monumenta vetustiora Arabiæ*, Lugd. Bat. 1740, where there will be found Fragments of Poetry *many Centuries before Mahomet*, and some said to be as antient *as the days of Solomon*.

† Vid. *Pocockii Not. in Camum Tograi*, p. 5.—and *Abulfed.* p. 194.

fortunate

fortunate for these last, that the *old Greeks* should have distinguished them by the same appellation †. C. VII.

If we reckon among pieces of Poetry not the *Metrical* only, but those also the mere efforts of *Invention* and *Imagination*, (such as the incomparable *Telemachus*, of the truly eloquent *Fenelon*) we may justly range in this Class, the *Arabian* Nights, and the *Turkish* Tales. They are valuable not only for exhibiting a picture of *Oriental* manners, during the splendor of the *Caliphate*, but for inculcating in many instances a useful and instructive *Moral*. Nothing can be better written than *the Tale of Alnaschar*, to illustrate that important part of the *Stoic Moral*, the fatal consequence *of not resisting our Fancies* *.

THEY

† See *Isocrates*, *Plato*, *Demosthenes*, &c.

* A curious and accurate Version of this admirable Tale is printed at *Oxford*, in a Grammar of the *Arabic* Lan-

P. III. They were fond of the *Fabulous* and *Allegorical*, and loved to represent under that Form the doctrines they most favoured. They favoured no doctrine more than that of each individual's *inevitable Destiny*. Let us see after what manner they conveyed this doctrine.

" They tell us that as *Solomon* (whom " they supposed a Magician from his superior Wisdom) was one day walking " with a person in *Palestine*, his Companion said to him with some horror, " *what ugly Being is that which approaches* " *us? I don't like his Visage—send me, I* " *pray thee, to the remotest Mountain of* " *India.*" *Solomon* complied, and the very " moment he was sent off, the *ugly* Being

Language; a Version which gives us too much reason to lament our imperfect view of those other ingenious Fictions, so *obscurely* transmitted to us thro' a *French Medium*.

" arrived:

"arrived. "*Solomon* (said the Being) *how* "*came that fellow* HERE? *I was to have* "*fetched him from the remotest Mountain* "*of India.*" *Solomon* anſwered—"ANGEL "OF DEATH, *thou wilt find him* THERE*."

I may add to this that elegant Fiction concerning the *ſelf-taught* Philoſopher *Hai Ebn Yokdan*, who, being ſuppoſed to have been caſt an Infant on a deſert Iſland, is made by various Incidents (ſome poſſible, but all ingenious) to aſcend gradually, as he grew up *in Solitude*, to the Sublime of all Philoſophy, Natural, Moral, and Divine †.

BUT this laſt was the Production of a more refined Period, when they had adopted-

* This Tale was told me by Dr. *Gregory Sharpe*, late Maſter of the Temple, well known for his knowlege in *Oriental Literature*.

† See *Pococke's* Edition of this Work, Oxon. 1671.

ed

P. III. ed the Philosophy of other nations. In their earlier days of Empire they valued no Literature, but their own, as we have learnt from the celebrated Story, already related, concerning *Omar*, *Amrus*, and the Library at *Alexandria**.

The same *Omar*, after the same *Amrus* had conquered the vast Province of *Egypt*, and given (according to the custom of those early times) many proofs of *personal* strength and valour, the same *Omar* (I say) was desirous to see the Sword, by which *Amrus* had performed so many Wonders. Having taken it into his hand, and found it no better than any other sword, he returned it with contempt, and averred, *it was good for nothing. You say true, Sir*, replied *Amrus*; *for you demanded to see the Sword, not the Arm that wielded it*;

* See before, p. 252. 322.

it; while that was wanting, the Sword was no better than the sword of Pharezdacus. C. VII

Now *Pharezdacus* was it seems a Poet, famous for his *fine description* of a Sword, but not equally famous for his *personal Prowess* *.

'Tis a singular instance of their attention to *Hospitality*, that they used to kindle Fires by night, upon Hills near their Camps, to conduct wandering Travellers to a place of refuge †.

Such an attention to this Duty naturally brings to our mind what *Eumæus* in *the Odyssey* says to *Ulyssus*.

Ξεῖν' ἔ μοι θέμις ἔς', ἐδ' εἰ κακίων σέθεν ἔλθοι,
Ξεῖνον ἀτιμῆσαι, πρὸς γὰρ Διός εἰσιν ἅπαντες
Ξεῖνοι——

* *Pocock. Notæ in Carm. Togr.* p. 184.

† *Ejusd. Carm. Tograi*, p. 111.

STRANGER,

P III.

STRANGER, I dare not with dishonour treat
A STRANGER, tho' a worse, than thou, should come;
For STRANGERS all belong to Jove—

Οδυσ. Ξ. 56.

NOR are there wanting other instances of Resemblance to the age of *Homer*. When *Ibrahim*, a dangerous competitor of the Caliph *Almanzur*, had in a decisive battle been mortally wounded, and his friends were endeavouring to carry him off, a desperate conflict ensued, in which the Enemy prevailed, overpowered his Friends, and gained what they contended for, the Body of *Ibrahim*. The resemblance between this Story, and that respecting the Body of *Patroclus*, is a fact too obvious, to be more than hinted *.

IN an earlier period, when *Moawigea* (the competitor of the great *Ali*) was prest

* See *Abulfeda*, p. 148.

in

in a battle, and had juſt begun to fly, he is reported to have rallied upon the ſtrength of certain verſes, which at that critical inſtant occured to his memory. The Verſes were theſe, as we attempt to tranſlate them.

When direful Scenes of Death appear,
And fill thy flutt'ring Heart with fear:
Say—HEART! *be firm; the ſtorm endure;*
For Evils ever find a cure.
Their Mem'ry, ſhould we 'ſcape, will pleaſe;
*Or, ſhould we fall, we ſleep at eaſe**.

THIS naturally ſuggeſts to every Lover of *Homer*, what is ſaid by *Ulyſſes*.

Τέτλαθι δὴ κραδίη· καὶ κύντερον ἄλλο ποτ᾽ ἔτλης
Ἤματι τῷ, ὅτε, κ. τ. λ. Οδυσ. Υ΄. 18.

Indure it, HEART; *for worſe thou haſt indured*
In days of yore, when &c.

* *Abulfeda*, p. 91.

P. III. SUCH Resemblances, as these, prove a probable connection between the manners of the *Arabians*, and those of the antient *Greeks*. There are other Resemblances, which, as they respect not only *Greek* Authors but *Roman*, are perhaps no more than *casual*.

THUS an *Arabian* Poet—

Horses and Wealth we know you've none;
Let then your Eloquence atone
*For Fortune's failure**——

WHAT the *Arabian* says of his Friend, *Horace* says of himself.

Donarem pateras, grataque commodus,
Censorine, meis &c. Od. L.

ANOTHER of their Poets has the following Sentiment.

* *Abulfeda*, p. 279.

Who

C. VII.

Who fondly can himself deceive,
And venture Reason's rules to leave;
Who dares, thro' ignorance, aspire
To that, which no one can acquire;
To spotless fame, to solid health,
To firm, unalienable, wealth:
Each Wish he forms, will surely find
A Wish denied to human kind.*

Here we read *the Stoic* Description of *Things not in our power*, and the consequence of pursuing them, as if they were *Things in our power*, concerning which fatal mistake see *Epictetus*, either in the Original, or in Mrs. *Carter*'s valuable Translation. The *Enchiridion* we know begins with this very doctrine.

There is a fine Precept among the *Arabians*—*Let him, to whom* the Gate

* *Abulfeda*, p. 279.

P. III. *of Good Fortune is opened, ſeize his Opportunity; for he knoweth not, how ſoon it may be ſhut.*

COMPARE this with thoſe admired Lines in *Shakſpeare*—

There is A TIDE *in the affairs of men,*
Which taken at the flood, &c.
Jul. Cæſ. Act IV. Sc. 5.

THO' the *Metaphors differ,* the *Sentiment* is *the ſame**.

IN the Comment on the Verſes of *Tograi* we meet an *Arabic* Sentiment, which ſays, that *a Friend is another ſelf.* The ſame elegant thought occurs in *Ariſtotle*'s Ethics, and that in the ſame words. Ἔστι γὰρ ὁ φίλος ἄλλος αὐτός.†

* *Bohadin Vit. Salad.* p. 73. Of this Work, p. 169.

† *Ariſt. Ethic. Nicom.* X. 4. and *Not. in Carm. Tograi,* p. 25.

AFTER

AFTER the preceding inſtances of *Arabian* Genius, the following perhaps may give a ſample of their *Manners* and *Character*. C. VII.

ON a rainy day the *Caliph Almotaſem* happened, as he was riding, to wander from his attendants. While he was thus alone, he found an old Man, whoſe Aſs, laden with faggots, had juſt caſt his burden, and was mired in a ſlough. As the old Man was ſtanding in a ſtate of perplexity, *the Caliph* quitted his horſe, and went to helping up the Aſs. *In the name of my father and my mother, I beſeech thee*, ſays the old Man, *do not ſpoil thy cloaths. That is nothing to Thee*, replied the Caliph, who, after having helped up the Aſs, replaced the faggots, and waſhed his hands, got again upon his horſe, the old Man in the mean time crying out, *Oh Youth, may God reward thee!* Soon after this the Caliph's com-

P. III. pany overtook him, whom he generously commanded to present the old Man with a noble largess of gold*.

To this instance of *Generosity* we subjoin another of *Resentment*.

The *Grecian Emperors* used to pay the *Caliphs* a tribute. This the Emperor *Nicephorus* would pay no longer; and not only that, but requiring the *Caliph* in a haughty manner to refund all he had received, added that, if he refused, the Sword should decide the Controversy. The Caliph had no sooner read the Letter, than inflamed with rage he inscribes upon the back of it the following answer.

In the name of the most merciful God: from Harun, Prince of the Faithful, to Nicephorus, Dog of the Romans: I have

* *Abulpharagius*, p. 166.

read

read thy Epistle, Thou Son of an unbelieving Mother: to which, what thou shalt BEHOLD, *and not what thou shalt* HEAR, *shall serve for an answer.* C. VII.

He immediately upon the very day decamped; marched as far as *Heraclia*, and, filling all things with rapine and slaughter, extorted from *Nicephorus* the performance of his Contract *.

The following is an instance of a calmer *Magnanimity*. In the middle of the third Century after *Mahomet*, one *Jacub*, from being originally a Brazier, had made himself Master of some fine Provinces, which he governed at will, tho' professing (like the Eastern Governors of later times) a seeming deference to his proper Sovereign.

* *Abulfeda*, p. 166, 167.

P. III. THE *Caliph*, not satisfied with this apparent submission, sent a Legate to persuade him into a more perfect obedience. *Jacub*, who was then ill, sent for the Legate into his presence, and there shewed him three things, which he had prepared for his inspection; a Sword, some black Barley Bread, and a Bundle of Onions. He then informed the Legate, that, should he die of his present disorder, the Caliph in such case would find no farther trouble. But if the contrary should happen, there could be then no Arbitrator to decide between them, excepting *that*, pointing to the *Sword*. He added, that if Fortune should prove adverse, should he be conquered by the Caliph, and stripped of his possessions, he was then resolved to return to his antient frugality, pointing to the *Black Bread* and the *Bundle of Onions* *.

---

* *Abulfeda*, p. 214.

To

2. To former inſtances of *Munificence* we add the following, concerning the celebrated *Almamun* *.

BEING once at *Damaſcus*, and in great want of money, he complained of it to his Brother *Mottaſem*. His Brother aſſured him he ſhould have money in a few days, and ſent immediately for thirty thouſand pieces of Gold from the revenues of thoſe Provinces, which he governed in the name of his Brother. When the money arrived, brought by the Royal beaſts of burden, *Almamun* invited *Jahia* the Son of *Actam*, one of his favourites, to attend him on horſeback, and view what was brought. They went accordingly, and beheld the Treaſure arranged in the fineſt order, and the Camels too, which had brought it, richly decorated. The Prince admired both the quantity

* See p. 326.

of

P. III. of the money, and the elegance of the shew; and as his Courtiers looked on with no less admiration, *he bid them be of good cheer.* Then turning about to *Jahia: O! Abu Mohammed,* says he, *we should be sordid indeed, were we to depart hence with all this money, as if it were scraped up for ourselves alone, whilst our longing friends look on to no purpose.* Calling therefore immediately for a Notary, he commands him to write down for such a family so many thousands; for such a family so many; and so on, never stopping till, out of the thirty thousand pieces, he had given away twenty-four thousand, without so much as taking his foot out of the stirrup *.

From *Munificence* we pass to another Quality, which, tho' less amiable, is not less striking and popular, I mean *Magnificence.*

---

* *Abulfeda,* p. 189.

C. VII.

The ſplendour of the Caliph *Moctader*, when he received the Ambaſſador of the *Greek Emperor* at *Bagdad*, ſeems hardly credible. We relate it from one of their Hiſtorians, preciſely as we find it.

The Caliph's whole Army both Horſe and Foot were under Arms, which together made a Body of one hundred and ſixty thouſand Men. His State-officers ſtood near him in the moſt ſplendid apparel, their Belts ſhining with Gold and Gems. Near them were ſeven thouſand Eunuchs; four thouſand white, the remainder of them black. The Porters or Door-keepers were in number ſeven hundred. Barges and Boats with the moſt ſuperb decoration were ſwimming on the *Tigris*. Nor was the Palace itſelf leſs ſplendid, in which were hung up thirty-eight thouſand pieces of Tapeſtry; twelve thouſand five hundred of which were of ſilk, embroidered with gold. The Carpets on the floor were twenty-two thou-

P. III. thousand. An hundred Lions were brought out, with a Keeper to each Lion.

Among the other Spectacles of rare and stupendous luxury, was a Tree of Gold and Silver, which opened itself into eighteen larger branches, upon which, and the other less branches, sate Birds of every sort, made also of gold and silver. The Tree glittered with Leaves of the same Metals, and while its branches thro' Machinery appeared to move of themselves, the several Birds upon them warbled their proper and natural notes.

When the *Greek* Ambassador was introduced to the *Caliph*, he was led by the Visir thro' all this *Magnificence* *.

But besides *Magnificence* of this kind, which was at best but *temporary*, the

* *Abulfeda*, p. 237. This, according to the *Christian Æra*, happened in the year 917.

Caliphs

C. VII.

Caliphs gave inſtances of *Grandeur* more *permanent*. Some of them provided public buildings for the reception of Travellers; ſupplied the Roads with Wells and Watering Places; meaſured out the diſtances by columns of Stone, and eſtabliſhed Poſts and Couriers. Others repaired old Temples, or built magnificent new ones. The proviſion of Snow (which in hot Countries is almoſt a Neceſſary) was not forgotten. Add to this Forums, or public Places for Merchants to aſſemble; Infirmaries; Obſervatories, with proper Inſtruments, for the uſe of Aſtronomers; Libraries, Schools, and Colleges for Students; together with Societies, inſtituted for Philoſophical inquiry*.

In

---

* Many things are enumerated in this Paragraph, to confirm which we ſubjoin the following References among many omitted.

For *Buildings to accommodate Travellers*, *Abulfed.* p. 154. *Abulphar.* p. 315, 316.

For

P. III. In the account of the *Escurial Arabic* Manuscripts, lately given by the learned *Casiri*, it appears that the *Public* Libraries in *Spain*, when under the *Arabian* Princes, were no fewer than seventy: a noble help

---

For *Wells upon the Road, Watering-places* and *Mile-stones*, *Abulfed.* p. 154. for *Posts and Couriers*, the same, p. 157. 283.

For *Temples*, *Abulfed.* p. 125. *Abulphar.* p. 210, 315, 316.

For *Snow*, *Abulfed.* p. 154. *Abulphar.* p. 261. *Bohadin*, p. 70.

For *Infirmaries*, *Abulphar.* p. 210. 343.

For *Observatories*, *Public Schools*, &c. *Abulphar.* p. 216.

For *Learned Societies*, *Abulphar.* p. 217. *Abulfed.* p. 181, 182, 183. 210. 274. *Bohadin Vit. Salad.* p. 25.

Among their Philosophical Transactions was a Mensuration of the Earth's Circumference, made by order of the Caliph *Almamun*, which they brought to about twenty-four thousand Miles.

this

this to Literature, when Copies of Books were ſo rare and expenſive*. C. VII.

A tranſaction between one of the Caliph of *Bagdad's* Ambaſſadors and the Court of *Conſtantinople*, is here ſubjoined, in order to illuſtrate the then *Manners* both of the Ambaſſador and the Court.

As this Court was a remnant of the antient Imperial one under the *Cæſars*, it ſtill retained (as was natural) after its dominions were ſo much leſſened, an attachment to that Pomp and thoſe minute Ceremonials, which in the zenith of its Power it had been able to enforce. 'Twas an Affection for this ſhadow of Grandeur, when the ſubſtance was in a manner gone, that induced the Emperor *Conſtantine Porphyrogenitus*

* Vid. *Biblioth. Arabico-Hiſpan.* Vol II. p. 71. *Matriti*, 1770.

P. III. *phyrogenitus* to write no leſs than a large Folio Book upon its Ceremonials *.

'TWAS in conſequence of the ſame principles, that the above Ambaſſador, tho' coming from the *Caliph*, was told to make a humble obeiſance, as he approached the *Grecian* Emperor. This the Ambaſſador (who had his *national* pride alſo) abſolutely refuſing, it was ingeniouſly contrived, that he ſhould be introduced to the Emperor thro' a door ſo very low, as might oblige him, however unwillingly, to make the Obeiſance required. The Ambaſſador, when he arrived, no ſooner ſaw the door, than he comprehended the contrivance, and with great readineſs turned about, and entered the Room backward †.

---

* See before, p. 299.

† *Abulphar.*

C. VII.

We have ſaid little concerning eminent ARABIANS during this period in SPAIN. Yet that we may not be wholly ſilent, we ſhall mention one fact concerning AVERROES, the famous Philoſopher and Lawyer, who was born at *Corduba* in the eleventh Century.

As he was lecturing one day in the College of Lawyers, a Slave, belonging to one who was his Enemy, came and whiſpered him. AVERROES turning round, and ſaying, *well, well,* the company believed the Slave had brought him a meſſage from his maſter. The next day the Slave returned, implored his pardon, and publicly confeſſed that, when he whiſpered him, he had ſpoken a ſlander. *God forgive thee,* replied AVERROES; *Thou haſt publicly ſhewn me to be a patient man; and as for thy injury, 'tis not worthy of notice.* AVERROES after this gave him money, adding withal this monition:

P. III. *What thou hast done to* ME, *do not do to another* *.

AND here, before we conclude this Chapter, we cannot help confessing that the *Facts*, we have related, are not always arranged in the strict order of *Chronology*.

THE MODES indeed of *History* (if these Chapters merit that name) appear to be different. *There is a Mode* which we may call Historical *Declamation*; a *Mode*, where the Author, dwelling little upon *Facts*, indulges himself in various and copious *Reflections*.

WHATEVER Good (if any) may be derived from this Method, it is not likely to give us much Knowledge of *Facts*.

† *Fabric. Biblioth. Græc.* T. XIII. p. 283, 284.

Another

Another Mode is that, which I call *General* or rather *Public* Hiſtory; a *Mode*, abundant in *Facts*, where Treaties and Alliances, Battles and Sieges, Marches and Retreats are accurately retailed; together with Dates, Deſcriptions, Tables, Plans, and all the collateral helps both of *Chronology* and *Geography*. C. VII.

In this, no doubt, there is Utility. Yet *the ſameneſs* of the Events reſembles not a little the Sameneſs of Human Bodies. One Head, two Shoulders, two Legs, &c. ſeem equally to characteriſe an *European* and an *African*; a native of *old Rome*, and a native *of Modern*.

A third Species of Hiſtory ſtill behind is that, which gives a ſample of Sentiments and Manners.

If the account of *theſe laſt* be faithful, it cannot fail being inſtructive, ſince we view thro' theſe *the interiour of human Na-*

 ture.

 ture. 'Tis by these we perceive what sort of animal *Man* is; so that while not only *Europeans* are distinguished from *Asiatics*, but *English* from *French*, *French* from *Italians*, and (what is still more) every individual from his neighbour: we view at the same time ONE NATURE, *which is common to them all.*

Horace informs us that a *Drama*, where the SENTIMENTS and MANNERS are well preserved, will please the Audience more than a POMPOUS FABLE, where they are *wanting**. Perhaps, what is true in *Dramatic* Composition, is not less true in *Historical.*

PLUTARCH, among the *Greek* Historians, appears in a peculiar manner to have merited this praise. So likewise BOHADIN among the *Arabians*, and to Him

* Sup. p. 212. in the Note.

we

we add ABUL-PHARAGIUS, and ABUL-FEDA, from whom ſo many facts in theſe Chapters are taken. C. VII.

NOR ought I to omit (as I ſhall ſoon refer to them) ſome of our beſt MONKISH HISTORIANS, tho' prone upon occaſion to degenerate into *the incredible.* As they often lived during the times which they deſcribed, 'twas natural they ſhould paint *the life* and THE MANNERS, which *they ſaw.*

A SINGLE Chapter more will finiſh all we have to ſay concerning the *Arabians.*

CHAP. VIII.

ARABIANS *favoured* MEDICINE *and* ASTROLOGY—*facts, relative to these two subjects—they valued* KNOWLEDGE, *but had no Ideas of* CIVIL LIBERTY—*the mean Exit of their last Caliph,* MOSTASSEM—*End of their Empire in* ASIA, *and in* SPAIN—*their present wretched degeneracy in* AFRICA—*an Anecdote.*

THE ARABIANS favoured MEDICINE and ASTROLOGY, and many of their Princes had Professors of each sort usually near their persons. *Self-Love*, a natural Passion, led them to respect the Art of Healing; *Fear*, another natural Passion, made them anxious to know *the Future*, and *Superstition* believed there were men, who, by *knowing the Stars*, could discover it.

WE

WE shall first say something concerning MEDICINE*, which we are sorry to couple with so futile an imposture. C.VIII.

'TIS commonly supposed that *the Prescriber* of Medicines, and *the Provider*, that is to say in common words, *the Physician* and *the Apothecary*, were characters anciently *united* in *the same* person. The following fact proves the contrary, at least among *the Orientals*.

IN an Army commanded by *Aphshen*, an Officer of the *Caliph Al-Motassem*, it happened that *Aphshin* and the Army Physician, *Zacharias*, were discoursing together. *I assert*, says *Zacharias*, *you can send for nothing from an Apothecary, but, whether he has it or has it not, he will affirm that he has. Aphshin*, willing to make the trial, bids them bring him a catalogue of unknown *people*, and transcribing out of it

* *Abulphar*. p. 160.

P. III. about twenty of their *names*, sends Messengers to the Apothecaries to provide him those Medicines. A few confest they knew no such medicines; others affirmed *they knew them well*, and taking the money from the Messengers, gave them something out of their shops. *Aphshin* upon this, called them together, permitted those, who said they knew nothing of the Medicines, to remain in the Camp, and commanded the rest that instant to depart *.

The following story is more interesting.

The Caliph, *Mottawakkell*, had a Physician belonging to him, who was a CHRISTIAN, named *Honaïn*. One day, after some other incidental conversation, *I would have thee*, says the Caliph, *teach me a Prescription, by which I may take off any*

* *Abulphar.* p 167.

Enemy

Enemy I please, and yet at the same time it should never be discovered. Honaïn, declining to give an answer, and pleading ignorance, was imprisoned. C.VIII.

BEING brought again, after a year's interval, into the *Caliph*'s presence, and still persisting in his ignorance, tho' threatened with death, the *Caliph* smiled upon him and said, *Be of good cheer, we were only willing to try thee, that we might have the greater confidence in thee.*

As *Honaïn* upon this bowed down and kissed the Earth, *What hindered thee,* says the *Caliph, from granting our request, when thou sawest us appear so ready to perform what we had threatened? Two things,* replied *Honaïn,* MY RELIGION, *and* MY PROFESSION; MY RELIGION, *which commands me to do good to my Enemies;* MY PROFESSION, *which was purely instituted for the benefit of Mankind.* TWO NOBLE

LAWS,

P. III. LAWS, ſaid the *Caliph*, and immediately preſented him (according to the Eaſtern Uſage) with rich garments and a ſum of money *.

THE ſame *Caliph* was once ſitting upon a Bench with another of his Phyſicians, named *Bactiſh*, who was dreſt in a Tunic of rich ſilk, but which happened on the edge to have a ſmall Rent. The *Caliph*, entering into diſcourſe with him, continued playing with this rent, till he had made it reach up to his girdle. In the courſe of their converſation, the *Caliph* aſked him, *How he could determine, when a Perſon was ſo mad, as to require being bound?*—*We bind Him,* replies *Bactiſh*, *when things proceed to that extremity, that he tears the Tunic of his Phyſician up to the girdle.* The *Caliph* fell backward in a fit of laughing, and ordered *Bactiſh* (as

* *Abulpharag.* p. 172, 173.

he

C. VIII.

he had ordered *Honaïn*) a Present of rich Garments, and a Donation in Money *.

THAT ſuch Freedom of Converſation was not always checked, may appear from the following, as well as the preceding Narrative.

THE *Caliph*, *Al-wathick*, was once fiſhing with a rod and line, upon a Raft in the River *Tigris*. As he happened to catch nothing, he turned about to his Phyſician *John, the Son of Miſna*, then ſitting near him, and ſaid a little ſharply, *Thou unlucky fellow, get thee gone. Commander of the Faithful*, replies his Phyſician; *ſay not what is abſurd. That John, the Son of Miſna, whoſe Father was an obſcure Man, and whoſe Mother was purchaſed for a few pieces of Silver; whom Fortune has ſo far favoured, that he has*

* *Abulpharag.* p. 171.

P. III. *been admitted to the ſociety and familiarity of Caliphs; who is ſo overpowered with the good things of life, as to have obtained from them that, to which even his hopes did not aſpire; that* HE (I ſay) *ſhould be an* UNLUCKY FELLOW, *is ſurely ſomething moſt abſurd.*—

However, if the Commander of the Faithful would have me tell him, WHO IS UNLUCKY, *I will inform him.—And who is he,* ſays the *Caliph?—The Man,* replied JOHN, *who being ſprung from four Caliphs, and being then raiſed thro' God to the Caliphate* HIMSELF, *can leave his Caliphate and his Palaces, and in the middle of the Tigris ſit upon a paultry raft twenty cubits broad, and as many long, without the leaſt aſſurance that a ſtormy blaſt may not ſink him; reſembling too by his employ the pooreſt, the worſt fellows in the world, I mean Fiſhermen.*——

THE

C.VIII.

The Prince on this ſingular diſcourſe only remarked—*My Companion I find is moved, if my preſence did not reſtrain him* *.

Another inſtance of lenity I muſt not omit, tho' in a later period, and in another Country. When *Al-azis* was Sultan of Egypt, a Poet there wrote a ſcandalous invective upon *Him* and *his Vizir*. The Vizir complained and repeated the Verſes to *Al-azis*, to whom the Sultan thus replied: *I perceive*, ſays he, *that in this invective* I *have my ſhare along with* You: *in pardoning it*, you *ſhall have your ſhare along with* Me †.

We are now, as we promiſed, to mention Astrology, which ſeems to have been connected in its origin with *Aſtronomy*. Philoſophers, men of veracity,

* *Abulpharag.* p. 168.

† *Abulpharag.* p. 219.

ſtudied

P. III. ſtudied the Heavenly Bodies; and 'twas upon *their* labours, that Impoſtors built *Aſtrology*.

The Following Facts however, notwithſtanding its temporary credit, ſeem not much in its favour.

When *Al-wathick* (the *Caliph*, whom we have juſt mentioned) was dangerouſly ill, he ſent for *his Aſtrologers*, one of whom, pretending to inquire into his deſtiny, pronounced that from that day he would live fifty years. He did not however live beyond ten days *.

A few years after, the ſame Pretenders to Prediction ſaid, that a vaſt number of Countries would be deſtroyed by floods; that the Rains would be immenſe, and

* *Abulpharag.* p. 168.

the

the Rivers far exceed their usual boundaries. C.VIII.

Men began upon this to prepare; to expect Inundations with terror; and to betake themselves into places, which might protect them by their altitude.

The Event was far from corresponding either to the *threats* of the Prophets, or to the *fears* of the Vulgar. The Rain that season was so remarkably small, and so many Springs and Rivers were absorbed by the Drought, that Public Supplications for Rain were many times made in the City of *Bagdad**.

We must however confess that notwithstanding these and many other such failures, *Astrologers* still maintained their

* *Abulpharag*. p. 181. *Abulfeda*, p. 222.

ground,

P. III. ground, gained admittance for many years into the Courts of theſe Princes, and were conſulted by many, who appear not to have wanted abilities.

As the *Weſt* of *Europe* learnt *Aſtronomy* from theſe *Arabians*, ſo ASTROLOGY appears to have attended it, and to have been much eſteemed during Centuries not remote, thro' *Germany*, *Italy*, *France*, &c.

EVEN ſo late as the days of Cardinal *Mazarine*, when that Miniſter lay on his death-bed, and a Comet happened to appear, there were not wanting Flatterers to inſinuate, that it had reference to *Him*, and his deſtiny. The Cardinal anſwered them with a manly pleaſantry—"*Meſ-*"*ſieurs, la Comete me fait trop d'hon-*"*neur**."

* *Bayle, ſur la Comete.*

WE

C.VIII.

We cannot quit these Orientals without observing that, tho' they eagerly coveted the fair Fruit of Knowlege, they appear to have had little relish for the fairer Fruit of Liberty. This valuable Plant seems to have rarely flourished beyond the bounds of *Europe*, and seldom even there, but in *particular* regions.

It has appeared indeed from the facts already alleged, that these *Eastern* Princes often shewed many eminent Virtues; the Virtues I mean of Candour, Magnanimity, Affability, Compassion, Liberality, Justice, and the like. But it does not appear, that either *they* or their *subjects* ever quitted those ideas of *Despotism* and *Servitude*, which during all ages appear to have been *the Characteristic* of *Oriental* Dominion.

As all things human naturally decay, so, after a period of more than five Centuries, did the illustrious race of the Abas-

P. III. SIDÆ. The laſt reigning Caliph of that Family, *Al-Moſtaſſem*, waſting his time in idleneſs and luxury, and that without the leaſt Judgment, or Conſiſtency in the conduct of his Empire; when he was told of the formidable approach of the *Tartars*, and how neceſſary it was, either to ſooth them by Submiſſion, or to oppoſe them by Force, made, in anſwer to this advice, the following mean reply—*For* ME *Bagdad ſuffices; which they will not ſurely think too much, if I yield them the other Provinces. They will not invade me, while I remain there; for this is my Manſion, and the place of my abode.*

LITTLE did theſe poor Sentiments avail. *Bagdad* ſoon after was taken, and he himſelf, having baſely aſked permiſſion to approach the *Tartar* Prince, appeared, and offered him diſhes, filled with Pearls and precious Stones. Theſe *the Tartar* diſtributed among his Attendants, and a few days

days after put the unhappy *Caliph* to death*.

Bagdad being loſt, by this fatal Event the *Dignity* and *Sovereignty* of the *Caliphs* were no more.

The Name indeed remained in *Egypt* under the *Mamlucs*, but it was a name merely of *Honour*, as thoſe other Princes were abſolute.

It even continued in the ſame Family to the time of *Selim*, Emperor of the *Turks*. When that Emperor in 1520 conquered *Egypt*, and deſtroyed the *Mamlucs*, he carried the *Caliph*, whom he found there, a Priſoner to *Conſtantinople*. 'Twas partly in this laſt City, and partly in *Egypt* that this *Caliph*, when degraded,

---

* *Abulpharag.* p. 318, 337, 338, 339. Theſe Events happened in the middle of the thirteenth Century.

P. III. lived upon a Penſion. When he died, the Family of THE ABASSIDÆ, once ſo illuſtrious, and which had borne the Title of *Caliph* for almoſt eight hundred years, ſunk with Him from Obſcurity into Oblivion *.

WHEN the *Tartars* and the *Turks* had extinguiſhed the Sovereignty of theſe *Arabians* in the Eaſt, and the Deſcendants of the antient *Spaniards* had driven them out of *Spain*, the remainder in *Africa* ſoon degenerated; till at length under the celebrated MULY ISMAEL, in the beginning of this Century, they ſunk into a State of *Ignorance*, *Barbarity*, and *abject* *Servi-*

* See the Supplement of that excellent Scholar, *Pococke*, to his Edition of *Abulpharagius*. In this Supplement we have a ſhort but accurate Account of the *Caliphs* who ſucceeded *Moſtaſem*, even to the time of their Extinction.

See alſo *Herbelot's Biblioth. Orientale*, under the Word *Abaſſides*, with the ſeveral references to other Articles in the ſame Work.

tude,

tude, hardly to be equalled either in antient or in modern Hiſtory. C.VIII.

But I ſay nothing concerning them during this unhappy Period. That which I have been treating, tho' in Chronology a *middle* Period, was to them, in many reſpects, a truly *Golden* one.

I conclude this Chapter with the following Anecdote, ſo far curious, as it proves that, even in our own Century, the Taſte among *the Orientals* for Philoſophy was not *totally* extinguiſhed.

In the year 1721 a Turkiſh Envoy came to the Court of *France*. As he was a Man of Learning, he ſearched thro' *Paris* (tho' in vain) for the Commentary of *Averroes upon Ariſtotle*, a large Work in *Latin*, containing five Folio Volumes, printed at *Venice* by the *Juntæ*, in the years 1552, 1553. It happened that, vi-

P. III. ſiting the King's Library, he ſaw the Book he wanted; and ſeeing it, he could not help expreſſing his ardent wiſh to poſſeſs it. The King of *France*, hearing what had happened, ordered the Volumes to be magnificently bound, and preſented him by his Librarian, the Abbe *Bignon* *.

---

* *Vid. Reimanni Hiſtor. Atheiſmi et Atheorum*, 8vo. p. 537.

CHAP.

CHAP. IX.

Concerning the LATINS *or* FRANKS—BEDE, ALCUIN, JOANNES ERIGENA, *&c.* GERBERTUS *or* GIBERTUS, *travelled to the Arabians in Spain for improvement—suspected of* MAGIC—*this the misfortune of many superior Geniuses in dark Ages; of* BACON, PETRARCH, FAUST, *and others*—*Erudition of* THE CHURCH; *Ignorance of* THE LAITY—INGULPHUS, *an Englishman, educated in the Court of Edward the Confessor—attached himself to the Duke of Normandy—accomplished Character of* QUEEN EGITHA, *Wife of the Confessor—Plan of Education in those Days*—THE PLACES *of Study*, THE AUTHORS *studied—Canon Law, Civil Law, Holy War, Inquisition—Troubadours*—WILLIAM OF POICTON—*Debauchery, Corruption, and Avarice of the Times*—

P. III.

WILLIAM THE CONQUEROR, *his Character and Taste—his Sons,* RUFUS *and* HENRY—*little Incidents concerning them* —HILDEBERT, *a Poet of the times*—*fine Verses of his quoted.*

I Pass now to another Race, THE LATINS, *or Inhabitants of* WESTERN EUROPE, who in this middle age were often by the *Arabians*, their Contemporaries, called FRANKS.

IGNORANCE was their *general* Character, yet *Individuals* we except in the enumeration, which follows.

BEDE, called *the Venerable* from his respectable Character, was *an Englishman*; was born, in the seventh Century, but flourished in the eighth; and left many Works, Critical, Historical, and Theological, behind him.

ALCUIN

Alcuin (ſometimes called *Alcuinus*, ſometimes *Flaccus Albinus*) was *Bede*'s Diſciple, and like him an *Engliſhman*. He was famous for having been Preceptor to *Charlemagne*, and much in his favour for many years*.

Joannes Erigena, a Native of *Scotland*, and who about the ſame period, or a little later lived ſometimes in *France*, and ſometimes in *England*, appears to have underſtood *Greek*, a rare accompliſhment for *thoſe* Countries in thoſe days.

It is related of him, that when he was once ſitting at table over againſt the Emperor, *Charles the Bald*, the Emperor

* The *Grammatical* Works of theſe two, together with thoſe of other Grammarians, were publiſhed in Quarto by *Putſchius*, at *Hanover*, in the year 1605. Thoſe, who would learn more concerning them, may conſult *Fabricius* and *Cave*.

aſked

P. III. aſked him—*How far diſtant* A SCOTT *was from* A SOTT?—*As far, Sir,* replied he, *as the Table's length* *.

A Treatiſe of his, which appears to be *Metaphyſical,* intitled *De Diviſione Naturæ,* was printed in a thin Folio at OXFORD, in the year 1681.

ADELARD, a Monk of *Bath,* for the ſake of *Mathematical* Knowlege travelled into *Spain, Egypt,* and *Arabia,* and tranſlated *Euclid* out of *Arabic* into *Latin,* about the year 1130. ROBERT OF READ-

---

* In the original, taken from *Roger de Hoveden, Annal. pars prior,* it is—*Quid diſtæt inter* SOTUM *et* SCOTUM?—The Anſwer was—*Tabula tantum.*

We have tranſlated SOTUM, SOTT, in order to preſerve the Emperor's dull Pun, tho' perhaps not quite agreeably to its proper meaning.

The word SCOTUM plainly decides the Country of this learned man, which ſome ſeem, without reaſon, to have doubted.

ING,

ING, a Monk, travelled into *Spain* on the same account, and wrote about the year 1143*. Ch. IX.

THEY found, by fatal experience, that little Information was to be had *at home*, and therefore ventured upon these perillous journies abroad.

GERBERTUS or GIBERTUS, a Native of *France*, flourished a little before them in the *tenth* Century, called, (tho' not on his account) *Sæculum obscurum, the dark Age.* His ardent Love for *Mathematical Knowlege* carried *Him* too from his own Country into *Spain*, that he might there learn Science from the learned *Arabians*.

AFTER an uncommon proficiency in the *Mathematics*, and after having re-

* See *Wallis's* Preface to his *Algebra*, *Fol. Lond.* 1685. p. 5.

commended

P. III. commended himself for his Learning and Abilities both to *Robert*, King of *France*, and to the Emperor *Otho*, he became first Archbishop of *Rheims*, then of *Ravenna*, and at length *Pope*, by the name of SYLVESTER THE SECOND.

HIS three capital Preferments being at *Rheims*, *Ravenna*, and *Rome*, each beginning with an R, gave occasion to the following barbarous Verse—

*Transit ab R Gerbertus ad R, post Papa viget R**.

'TIS singular that not his *Sacerdotal*, nor even his *Pontifical* Character could screen him from the imputation of MAGIC, incurred merely, as it should seem, from his *superior Ingenuity*.

---

* See *Brown's Fasciculus rerum expetendăr. et fugiendăr.* Vol. II. p. 83.

A Bishop

Ch. IX.

A Bishop *Otho*, who lived in the next Century, gravely relates of him, that he obtained the *Pontificate* by *wicked Arts*, for in his youth, when he was nothing more then a simple Monk, having left his Monastery, *he gave himself up wholly to the Devil*, on condition *he might obtain* that, which he desired.

SOON after this, the same Historian, having given an account of his gradual Rise, subjoins — that at length, *by the Devil's help*, he was made *Roman Pontiff*, but then it was upon *Compact*, that after his decease, he should wholly in *Body* and *Soul* belong to HIM, thro' whose frauds he had acquired *so great* a Dignity *.

A Car-

* *Hic* (scilicet Gerbertus) *malis artibus Pontificatum obtinuit, eo quod ab adolescentia, cum Monachus esset, relicto Monasterio, se totum Diabolo obtulit, modo quod optabat obtineret.* — And soon after, a short narrative of his Rise being given, the Historian subjoins — *Postremo Romanus*

P. III. A Cardinal *Benno*, of nearly the same age with this Bishop *Otho*, speaking of the same great man (*Gerbertus* I mean) informs us, *his Demon* had assured him, that he should not die, till he had celebrated Mass at *Jerusalem*—that *Gerbertus*, mistaking this for *the City* so called, unwarily celebrated Mass *at Rome*, in a *Church* called *Jerusalem*, and, being deceived by the *Equivocation of the Name*, met a sudden and a wretched end*.

As to these Stories, they are of that *vagabond* sort, which wander from Age to Age, and from Person to Person; which find their way into the Histories of distant periods, and are sometimes transferred from *Histories* to the *Theatre*.

Romanus Pontifex Diabolo adjuvante fuit constitutus; hâc tamen lege, ut post ejus obitum totus ILLIUS *in anima et corpore esset, cujus fraudibus tantam adeptus esset dignitatem.* See Bishop OTHO, in *Brown's Fasciculus*, just quoted, V. II. p. 88.

* See the same *Fascicul.* p. 88.

THE

Ch. IX.

The Jerusalem Tale may be found in *Shakspeare's* Henry the Fourth; and for the Compact, we have all seen it in the Pantomine of Dr. Faustus.

One thiug we cannot but remark: the dull Contemporaries of these superior Geniuses, not satisfied with referring their Superiority to Pre-eminence *merely natural*, recurred absurdly to Power *supernatural*, deeming nothing less could so far exceed themselves.

Such was the Case of *the able Scholar* just mentioned. Such, some centuries afterward, was the Case of Roger Bacon, of Francis Petrarch, of John Faust, and many others.

Bacon's Knowlege of Glasses, and of the *Telescope* in particular, made them apply to Him *literally*, what *Virgil* had said *poetically*—

Carmina vel Cœlo possunt deducere Lunam.

Vir-

P. III. VIRGIL himself had been foolishly thought a *Magician*, and therefore, because PETRARCH was delighted with the study of so capital an author, even PETRARCH also was suspected of MAGIC.

FOR JOHN FAUST, as he was either the Inventor, or among the first Practisers of the Art of *Printing*, 'tis no wonder the ignorant vulgar should refer to *Diabolical* Assistance a Power, which multiplied Books in a manner to them so incomprehensible.

THIS Digression has led us to Examples rather against *Chronological Order*; tho' all of them included within that Age, of which we are writing *. For the

* BACON lived in the thirteenth Century; PETRARCH, in the fourteenth; FAUST, in the fifteenth. See a curious Book of *Gabriel Naude*, a learned *Frenchman* of the last Century, intitled *Apologie pour les grand Hommes, accusées de* MAGIE.

honour

honour too of the CHURCH, theſe *falſly accuſed Geniuſes* were all of them *Eccleſiaſtics*. Indeed the reſt of *Weſtern Europe* was in a manner *wholly barbarous*, compoſed of ignorant *Barons*, and their more ignorant *Vaſſals*; men like *Homer's Cimmerians*,

Ἠέρι καὶ νεφέλῃ κεκαλυμμένοι ——

With Fog and Cloud envelop'd ——

FROM theſe we paſs, or rather go back, to INGULPHUS, an *Eccleſiaſtic*, and an *Hiſtorian*, valuable for having lived during an intereſting *Time*, and in intereſting *Places*.

HE was by birth an *Engliſhman*, and had been educated in the Court of *Edward the Confeſſor*; went thence to the Court of the *Duke of Normandy*, to whoſe favour he was admitted, and there preferred. Some time after this, when the ſucceſsful Ex-

P. III. pedition of that Duke had put him in possession of the *Crown of England*, the Duke (then *William the Conqueror*) recalled him from *Normandy*; took him into favour here, and made him at length *Abbot of Croyland*, where he died advanced in years *.

INGULPHUS tells us, that King *Edward*'s Queen, EGITHA, was admirable for her *Beauty*, her *literary Accomplishments*, and her *Virtue*.

He relates, that being a Boy he frequently saw *Queen Egitha*, when he visited his Father, in King *Edward*'s Court; —that many times when he met her, as he was coming from School, she used to dispute with him about his Learning, and

* See *Ingulphus's History*, in the Preface to the *Oxford* Edition of the year 1684. See also p. 75, of the Work itself.

his

his Verſes—that ſhe had a peculiar pleaſure to paſs from *Grammar* to *Logic*, in which ſhe had been inſtructed; and that, when ſhe had entangled him there with ſome ſubtle Concluſion, ſhe uſed to bid one of her Attendants give him two or three pieces of money, and carry him to the Royal Pantry, where he was treated with a Repaſt *. Ch. IX.

As to *the Manners of the times*, he tells us, that the whole Nation began to lay aſide the *Engliſh Cuſtoms*, and in many things to *imitate the Manners of the French*; all the Men of Quality to ſpeak *the Gallic Idiom* in their Houſes, as a high ſtrain of Gentility; to draw their Charters and public Inſtruments after the manner of *the French*; and in theſe and many other things *to be aſhamed of their own Cuſtoms* †.

* See the ſame *Ingulphus*, p 62.

† See the ſame Author, in the ſame page.

P. III. SOME years before the Conqueſt, *the Duke of Normandy* (whom INGULPHUS calls *moſt illuſtrious* and *glorious)* made a viſit to *England,* attended with a grand retinue. King *Edward* received him honourably, kept him a long while, carried him round to ſee *his Cities* and *Caſtles,* and at length ſent him home with many rich Preſents*.

INGULPHUS ſays, that at this time *Duke William* had no hopes of *the Succeſſion,* nor was any mention made of it; yet conſidering the Settlement of the Crown made upon him ſoon afterward, and the Reception he then found, this ſhould hardly ſeem probable.

KING *Edward,* according to INGULPHUS, had great merit in remitting the

* See the ſame Author, p. 65. 68.

DANE-

DANE-GELT, that heavy Tax imposed upon the people by the *Danish Usurpers*, his immediate Predecessors *. Ch. IX.

As to LITERARY MATTERS, it has appeared that *the Queen*, besides the usual Accomplishments of the times, (which she undoubtedly possest) had been instructed also in superior sorts of Knowlege. She may be supposed therefore to have surpast, not only *her own* Court, but perhaps other Courts *since*, as they have seldom more to boast, than the fashionable Polish.

FOR the LITERARY QUALIFICATIONS of our *Histôrian* himself, we perceive something of his Education in what we have already quoted from him. He is more particular afterwards, when he tells that he was first bred at *Westminster*, and then

* See the same Author, p. 65.

P. III. ſent to *Oxford*—that in the firſt he learnt *Grammar*, in the laſt he ſtudied *Ariſtotle* and *the Rhetoric of Cicero*:—that finding himſelf ſuperior to many of his Contemporaries, and diſdaining the littleneſs of his own Family, he left home, ſought the Palaces of Kings and Princes, &c. &c. 'Twas thus that, after a variety of Events, he became Secretary to *the Duke of Normandy*, afterwards *William the Conqueror*, and ſo purſued his Fortune, till he became *Abbot of Croyland**.

WE ſhall only remark on this Narrative, that WESTMINSTER and OXFORD ſeem to have been *deſtined to the ſame purpoſes then, as now*; that the Scholar at WESTMINSTER was to *begin*, and at OXFORD was to *finiſh*; a Plan of Education which ſtill exiſts; which is not eaſy to

* See the ſame Author, p. 73. 75.

be

be mended; and which can plead ſo antient and ſo uninterrupted a Preſcription. Ch. IX.

NEARLY the ſame time a Monk, by name GRATIAN, collecting the numerous Decrees of Popes and Synods, was the firſt who publiſhed a Body of CANON LAW*. 'Twas then alſo, or a little earlier, that *Amalfi*, a City of *Calabria*, being taken by the *Piſans*, they diſcovered there by chance an original MS. of *Juſtinian's* CODE, which had been in a manner unknown from the time of that Emperor †. This curious Book was brought to *Piſa*, and, when *Piſa* was taken by the *Florentines*, was transferred to *Florence*, and there has continued even to this day.

---

* This happened in the year 1157. See *Duck De Auctoritate Juris Civilis Romanor.* p. 66 88. Edit. Lond. 1679.

† See the ſame author, p 66.—*Amalfi* was taken by the *Piſans* in the year 1127.

P. III. And thus it was that by singular fortune the Civil and Canon Law, having been about the same time promulged, gradually found their way into most of the *Western* Governments, changing more or less their Municipal Laws, and changing with those Laws the very forms of their Constitutions.

'Twas soon after happened that *wild Enthusiasm*, which carried so many thousands from the *West* into the *East*, to prosecute what was thought, or at least called A Holy War *.

After the numerous Histories antient and modern of these Crusades, it would be superfluous to say more, than to observe that, by *repeating* them, men ap-

* It began in the year 1095. See *Fuller's Holy Warre*, Book I ch. 8 *William of Malmesbury*, Lib. IV, c. 2. among the *Scriptores post Bedam*.

pear

pear to have grown worſe; to have become more ſavage, and *greater barbarians.* It was ſo late as during one of the *laſt* of them, that theſe Cruſaders ſacked the *Chriſtian* City of *Conſtantinople* *, and that while *theſe* were committing unheard-of cruelties in that *Capital of Chriſtendom*, *another* party of them, *nearer home*, were employed in maſſacring the innocent *Albigeois* †.

So great was the zeal of Extirpation, that when one of theſe *home* Cruſades was going to ſtorm the City of *Bezieres*, a City filled with *Catholics*, as well as

* In the year 1204. See the ſame *Fuller*, B. III. chap. 17. and *Nicetas* the *Choniate*, already quoted at large, from p. 300 to p. 313.

† The Cruſades againſt them began in the year 1206; the Maſſacres were during the whole courſe of the war; ſee *Fuller's H. Warre*, B. III. from chap. 18 to ch. 22. eſpecially chap. 21. and *Moſheim's Church Hiſtory*, under the article *Albigenſes*.

Heretics,

P. III. *Heretics*, a ſcruple aroſe that, by ſuch a meaſure, *the Good* might periſh as well as *the Bad*. *Kill them all*, ſaid an able Sophiſt—*kill them all, and God will know his own* *.

To diſcover theſe *Albigeois*, the home Cruſades were attended by *a Band of Monks*, whoſe buſineſs was TO INQUIRE after Offenders, called *Heretics*. When the *Cruſade* was finiſhed, the *Monks*, like the Dregs of an empty Veſſel, ſtill remained, and deriving from *the Cruſade* their *Authority*, from the *Canon Law* their *judicial* Forms, became by *theſe two* (I mean *the Cruſade* and *Canon Law*) that formidable Court, THE COURT OF INQUISITION.

BUT in theſe latter events we rather anticipate, for they did not happen till

* *Tuez les tous: Dieu connoit ceux, qui ſont a lui.* Hiſtoire de Troubadours, Vol I. p. 193.

the

the beginning of *the thirteenth* Century, Ch. IX. whereas the first Crusade was towards the End of *the eleventh* *.

About the beginning of the eleventh Century, and for a Century or two after, flourished the Tribe of Troubadours, or Provençal Poets †; who chiefly lived in the Courts of those Princes, that had

---

* In the year 1095 or 1096. — *Fuller's H. Warre*, p. 21. And *William of Malmesbury*, before quoted, p. 409.

'Tis to be remarked, that these two Events, I mean the sacking of *Constantinople*, and the Massacres of the *Albigeois*, happened more than *a hundred years* after this *Holy War* had been begun, and after its *more splendid* Parts were *past*, that is to say, the taking of *Jerusalem*, the establishment of *a Kingdom* there, (which lasted eighty years) and the *gallant Efforts* of *Coeur de Leon* against *Saladin*. All against the *Saracens*, that followed, was languid, and, for the greater part of it, adverse.

† See a Work, 3 Vol. 12mo. intitled, *Histoire Litteraire de Troubadours*, printed at *Paris* 1774, where there is an ample detail both of them, and their Poems.

P. III. had Sovereignties in or near PROVENCE, where the *Provençal Language* was ſpoken. 'Twas in this Language they wrote, a Language, which, tho' obſolete now, was then eſteemed the beſt in Europe, being prior to the *Italian* of *Dante* and *Petrarch*.

THEY were called TROUBADOURS from *Trouver, to find* or *to invent**, like the *Greek Appellation*, POET, which means (we know) A MAKER.

THEIR Subjects were moſtly *Galantry* and *Love*, in which their *licentious* Ideas we are told were exceſſive. Princes did not diſdain † to be of their number, ſuch among others as our RICHARD COEUR DE LEON, and the celebrated WILLIAM, COUNT *of* POICTOU, who was a Contem-

* See *Hiſt. de Troub.* Vol. I. Diſcours prelim p. 25.

† See the ſame Work in the ſame page.

-porary

porary with *William the Conqueror* and his Sons. Ch. IX.

A Sonnet or two, made by RICHARD, are preſerved, but they are obſcure, and as far as intelligible, of little value *.

THE Sonnets of WILLIAM *of Poictou*, now remaining, are (as we are informed) of the moſt *licentious* kind, for a more *licentious man* never exiſted †.

HISTORIANS tell us, that near one of his Caſtles he founded a ſort of Abbey

* See *Hiſt. de Troub.* Vol. I. p. 54.

† See *Hiſt. de Troub.* Vol. I p. 7.

As to his famous Abbey or Nunnery, ſoon after mentioned, ſee the ſame Work, p. 3, 4. but more particularly and authentically, ſee *William of Malmeſbury*, a writer nearly contemporary, and from whom the Narrative here given is taken. The Paſſage in *Malmeſbury* begins with the words—*Erat tum Willielmus, Comes Pictavorum*, &c. &c. p. 96. Edit. Londin. Fol. 1596.

for

P. III. for Women of Pleaſure, and appointed the moſt celebrated among his Ladies to the Offices of Abbeſs, Prioreſs, &c. that he diſmiſt his Wife, and, taking the Wife of a certain Viſcount, lived with her publicly,—that being excommunicated for this by *Girard Biſhop of Angouleſme*, and commanded to put away his unlawful Companion, he replied, *Thou ſhalt ſooner curl Hair upon that bald Pate of thine, than will I ſubmit to a divorce from the Viſcounteſs*—that having received a like rebuke, attended with an Excommunication from his *own Biſhop, the Biſhop of Poictou*, he ſeized him by the Hair, and was about to diſpatch him, but ſuddenly ſtopt by ſaying, *I have that Averſion to Thee, Thou ſhalt never enter Heaven thro' the aſſiſtance of* MY *Hand**.

* The Words in *Malmeſbury* are—*Nec cælum unquam intrabis meæ manus miniſterio.* P. 96.

If

IF I might be permitted to digreſs, I would obſerve that HAMLET has adopted preciſely *the ſame* ſentiment. When he declines the opportunity offered him *of killing the King at his Prayers*, he has the following Expreſſions among many others Ch.IX.

A Villain kills my Father, and for that
I, his ſole ſon, do this ſame Villain SEND
TO HEAV'N—*O!* THIS *is Hire and Salary*,
NOT REVENGE.—*Hamlet* Act III. Sc. X.

'TIS hard to defend ſo ſtrange a ſentiment either in HAMLET, or THE COUNT. We ſhall only remark that HAMLET, when he delivered it, was perfectly *cool*; THE COUNT, agitated *by impetuous Rage*.

This Count, as he grew older, became, as many others have done, from *a Profligate a Devotee*; engaged in one of the *firſt Cruſades*; led a large body of Troops into the Eaſt; from which however, after his Troops had been routed, and moſt of them

P. III. them destroyed, he himself returned with ignominy home*.

THE loose Gallantry of these *Troubadours* may remind us of the Poetry during the Reign of *our second Charles*—nor were the *Manners* of one *Court* unlike those of the other, unless that those of the Court of *Poictou* were more abandoned of the two.

BE that as it may, we may fairly I think conclude, if we compare the two Periods, there were Men as *wicked* during the *early* period, as during the *latter*, and not only so, but *wicked* in Vices of *exactly the same* Character.

IF we seek for Vices of *another* character, we read *at the same æra* concerning a neighbouring Kingdom to *Poictou*,

* See the same *William of Malmesbury*, p. 75. 84.

that

that "All the people of rank were so Ch. IX.
" blinded with AVARICE, that it might be
" truly said of them (according to JU-
" VENAL)

Not one regards the method, HOW HE GAINS,
But fix'd his Resolution, GAIN HE MUST.

" THE more they discoursed about " Right, the greater their Injuries. " Those, who were called the Justicia- " ries, were the Head of all Injustice. " The Sheriffs and Magistrates, whose " Duty was Justice and judgment, were " more atrocious than the very Thieves " and Robbers, and were more cruel " than others, even the most cruel. The " King himself, when he had leased his " Domains as dear, as was possible, trans- " ferred them immediately to another " that offered him *more*, and then again " to another, neglecting always his for-

P. III. "mer agreement, and labouring ſtill for "*bargains* that were greater, and more "profitable *."

Such were *the* good old times of good old England, (for 'tis of *England* we have been reading) during the reign of our Conqueror, William.

And yet if we meaſure Greatness (as is too often the caſe with *Heroes*) by any other Meaſure, than that of *Moral Rectitude*, we cannot but admit that he *muſt* have been Great, who could conquer a Country ſo much larger than his own, and tranſmit the permanent Poſſeſſion of it to his Family. The numerous

* See *Henrici Huntindonienſis Hiſtor. L. VII.* p. 312, *inter Scriptores poſt Bedam*—Edit. London, 1594, beginning from the Words, '*Principes omnes*,' &c. The Verſe from *Juvenal* is—

Unde habeat, quærit nemo, ſed oportet habere.

Norman Families, with which he filled this Island, and the very few *Saxon* ones, which he suffered to remain, sufficiently shew us the Extent of this Revolution. Ch. IX

As to his TASTE, (for 'tis *Taste* we investigate, as often as we are able) there is a curious Fact, related of him by JOHN OF SALISBURY, a learned Writer, who lived as early at the times of *Stephen* and *Henry the Second.*

THIS Author, informs us, that WILLIAM, after he was once settled in the peaceable possession of his Kingdom, sent Ambassadors to Foreign Nations, that they should collect for him, out of all the celebrated Mansions, whatever should appear to them *magnificent* or *admirable.*

OUR Author cannot help allowing that this was the laudable project of a great man, desirous of pouring into *his*

P. III. *own* Dominious all, that was excellent in *others* *.

It does not appear what these Rarities were, but it sufficiently shews *the Conqueror* to have had a Genius superior to the Barbarity of his Age.

One may imagine he was not ignorant of *Ovid*, and the antient *Mythology*, by his answer to *Philip* King of France.

William, as he became old, grew to an *unweildy* Bulk. The king of *France*,

---

* *Simile aliquid fecisse visus est Rex Anglorum* VILHELMUS PRIMUS, *cujus virtuti Normannia et tandem major Britannia cessit.. Assumpto namque regni diademate, et pace composita, legatos misit ad exteras nationes, ut a præclaris omnium domibus, quicquid eis magnificum aut mirificum videretur, afferrent. Defluxit ergo in insulam opulentam, et quæ fere sola bonis suis est in orbe contenta, quicquid magnificentiæ, imo luxuriæ potuit inveniri. Laudabile quidem fuit magni viri propositum, qui virtutes omnium orbi suo volebat infundere.* Joan. Sarisb. de *Nugis Curialium*, p. 480. Edit. Lugd. 8vo. 1595.

in

in a manner not very polite, aſked of him, (with reference to this bulk) "*When, as* "*he had been ſo long in breeding, he expected* "*to be brought to bed?*"—"*Whenever that* "*happens,*" replied *William,* "*it will be, as* "SEMELE *was, in Flames and Thunder.*" *France* ſoon after that felt his Devaſtations *. Ch. XI.

HIS Son RUFUS ſeems more nearly to have approached the character of the times.

WE have a Sample of his Manners in the following Narrative. Being immenſely fond of expence in dreſs, when one of his

* *Quærente,* ſc. *Philippo, numquidnam tandem pareret* GUILIELMUS, *qui tam diu geſſiſſet* UTERUM : *ſe pariturum, ſed inſtar* SEMÈLES, *reſpondit, cum flammis et fulmine. Pancıroll. Nova Reperta,* Tit. x. p. 219. Edit. Françofurt. 1631. See this fact ſomewhat differently told by *Matthew Paris,* p. 13. *Edit. Fol. London,* 1640. The devaſtations, here mentioned, are related in the ſame page.

P. III. attendants brought him new Shoes; and was putting them on, he demanded, "*How* "*much they cost?*"—"*Three Shillings, Sir,*" replied his Attendant —"*Son of a Whore,*" says Rufus,—"*at so pitiful a price to pro*"*vide Shoes for a King!—Go and purchase* "*me some for a mark of Silver* *."

Matthew Paris writes, that he was once told of a formidable dream, relative to his death, which had been dreamed by a certain Monk. Rufus, on hearing it, burst into laughter, and said, "*The Man's* "*a Monk, and Monk-like has dreamed, to* "*get a little money—give him a hundred* "*Shillings, that he may not think he has* "*been dreaming for nothing* †".

* *Will. of Malmesbury*, p. 69. The words of *Rufus* were—*Fili meretricis, ex quo habet Rex caligas tam exilis pretii! Vade et affer mihi emptas marcâ argenti.*

† *Matthew Paris*, p. 53. Rufus's words were—*Monachus est, & lucri causa monachiliter somniavit: da ei centum solidos, ne videatur inaniter somniasse.*

His

His Hiſtorian *Malmeſbury*, after having related other Facts of him, adds, *that he had neither Application enough, nor Leiſure, ever to attend to Letters**. Ch. IX.

It was not ſo with his Brother, *Henry* the Firſt. He (as this Hiſtorian informs us †) ſpent his Youth in the ſchools of liberal Science, and ſo greedily imbibed the ſweets of *Literature*, that in aftertimes, (as the ſame Writer rather *floridly* relates) *no Tumults of War, no Agitation of Cares, could ever expel them from his illuſtrious Mind.*

Soon after we meet the well known ſaying of *Plato*, that 'twas then States would be happy, if *Philoſophers* were to reign, or *Kings* were to philoſophize. Our Hiſtorian, having given this Sentiment,

* *William of Malmeſbury*, p. 70.

† The ſame, p. 87.

P. III. tells us, (to use his own expressions) that *Henry* fortified his Youth with *Literature* in a view to the Kingdom, and ventured even in his Father's hearing, to throw out the Proverb, *Rex illiteratus, Asinus coronatus, that an illiterate King was but an Ass crowned* *.

THAT the King his Father, from perceiving his Son's Abilities, had something like *a Presentiment* of his future Dignity, may appear from the following Story.

WHEN *Henry* was young, one of his Brothers having injured him, he complained of his ill-treatment to his Father with tears. *Don't cry, Child,* says his Father, *for Thou too shalt be King* †.

---

* *William of Malmesbury*, p. 87, b.

* The Words of *William* were—*Ne fleas, Fili; quoniam et Tu Rex eris.* See the same Author in the same page, that is, p. 87. b.

As

Ch. IX.

As *Henry* was a learned Prince, we may suppose he was educated by learned men; and perhaps, if we attend to the account given by *Ingulphus* of his own Education * in the time of *Edward* the Confessor, 'tis probable there may have been *among the Clergy* a succession of learned men from the time of *Venerable Bede*.

'Tis certain that in *England at least*, during these *middle* Ages, Learning never flourished more, than from the time of *Henry the First* to the reign of his Grandson *Henry the second*, and for some years after.

The learned Historian of the Life of *Henry the Second* (I mean the First Lord Lyttelton) has put this beyond dispute.

Perhaps too *the Times, which followed*, were *adverse* to the Cause of Literature.

* P. 402, 405, 6.

P. III. THE CRUSADES had made the Laity greater Barbarians, if poſſible, than they were before. Their Cruelty had been ſtimulated by acting againſt *Greeks*, whom they hated for *Schiſmatics*; and againſt *Saracens*, whom they hated for *Infidels*; altho' it was from *theſe alone* they were likely to *learn*, had they underſtood (which *few* of them did) a ſyllable of *Greek* or *Arabic*.

ADD to this, THE INQUISITION being then * eſtabliſhed in all its terrors, *the Clergy* (from whom *only* the Cauſe of *Letters* could hope any thing) found their Genius inſenſibly checkt by its gloomy terrors.

THIS *depraved* Period (which laſted for a Century or two) did not mend, till *the Invention of Printing*, and the *Taking* of

---

* See before, p. 410.

Con-

Constantinople. Then 'twas that these, and other hidden Causes, roused the Genius of *Italy*, and restored to Mankind those *Arts* and that *Literature*, which to *Western Europe* had been so long unknown. Ch. IX.

Before I conclude this Chapter, I cannot but remark, that, during these inauspicious times, so *generally* tasteless, there were even Latins as well as Greeks *, whom *the very Ruins of Antique Arts* carried to *Enthusiastic Admiration*.

Hildebert, Arch-Bishop of *Tours*, who died in the year 1139, in a fine Poem, which he wrote upon the City of *Rome*, among others has the following Verses, in praise of the then remaining Statues and Antiquities.

Non tamen annorum series, nec flamma, nec
ensis,
Ad plenum potuit tale abolere decus.

---

* See before, what has been quoted from Nicetas the Choniate, p. 301, &c.

Hic

P. III.

Hic Superum formas Superi mirantur et ipsi,
Et cupiunt fictis vultibus esse pares.
Nec potuit Natura Deos hoc ore creare,
Quo miranda Deum signa creavit Homo.
Vultus adest his Numinibus, potiusque coluntur*
Artificum studio, quam Deitate sua †.

'Tis worth observing, that the *Latinity* of these Verses is in general pure, and that they are wholly free from the *Leonine jingle*.

They are thus attempted in *English* for the sake of those, who do not read the original.

But neither passing Years, nor Fire, nor Sword
Have yet avail'd such Beauty to annul.

* Forsan *Cultus.*

† *William of Malmesbury, p.* 76.—*Fabricii Bibliothca med. et infim. ætat. in voce* Hildebert.

Ev'n

Ev'n Gods themselves their mimic Forms admire,
And wish their own were equal to the feign'd.
Nor e'er could Nature Deities create
With such a Countenance, as Man has giv'n.
To these fair Statues, Creatures of his own.
Worship they claim, tho' more from HUMAN ART,
Than from THEIR OWN DIVINITY, *ador'd.*

CHAP.

CHAP. X.

SCHOOLMEN—*their Rise, and Character*—*their Titles of Honour*—*Remarks on such Titles*—ABELARD *and* HELOISA—JOHN *of* SALISBURY—*admirable Quotations from his two celebrated Works*—GIRALDUS CAMBRIENSIS—WALTER MAPES—RICHARD COEUR DE LEON—*his Transactions with Saladin*—*his Death, and the singular Interview, which immediately preceded it.*

WE are now to consider the state of LITERATURE with respect to *other* Geniuses, both before the *Conquest*, and after it, so low as to the times of our *First Richard*.

'TWAS during this Period began the Race of SCHOOLMEN, a Race much admired,

mired, and followed in their day. Their *ſubtlety* was great, and though that ſubtlety might ſometimes have led them into Refinements rather *frivolous*, yet have they given eminent ſamples of *penetrating Ingenuity*.

They began in the eleventh Century, and laſted to the fourteenth, when *new Cauſes* leading to *new Events*, they gradually decreaſed, and were no more.

That they had ſome merit muſt be allowed, when we are told that the learned Biſhop *Saunderſon* uſed conſtantly to read the Secunda Secundæ of Thomas Aquinas*, and that *this Treatiſe*, together with Aristole's Rhetoric, and Cicero's Offices were *three Books*, which he always had with him, and never ceaſed to peruſe. The *Scholaſtic* Tract muſt have

* This able and acute man died aged 48 years, in the year 1274.

P. III. been no bad one, which was so well asso-ciated.

Various Epithets at the time were bestowed upon these Schoolmen. There was *the Irrefragable* doctor, *the Subtle, the Seraphic, the Angelic,* &c.

There is certainly something exaggerated in the *Pomp* of these Appellations. And yet, if we reflect on our *modern* Titles of *Honour*; on our common *superscriptions* of *Epistles*; on our common modes of *concluding* them; and mark how *gravely* we admit all this: may we not suppose those *other* Epithets appear ridiculous, not so much from their being *absurd*, as from their being *unusual**?

Before we quit these *Schoolmen*, we

* For a fuller account of these *Schoolmen* see *Scholasticæ Theologiæ Syntagma*, by *Prideaux*, Bishop of Worcester, *Mosheim's* History, and *Cave's Histor. Lit.* V. 2. p. 275.

cannot

cannot omit the famous PETER ABELARD, who, when he taught at *Paris*, was followed by thousands, and was considered almost as an Oracle in discussing the abstrusest of subjects. At present he is better known for his unfortunate Amour with the celebrated HELOISA, his Disciple, his Mistress, and at length his Wife. Ch. X.

HER *Ingenuity* and *Learning* were celebrated also, and their *Epistolary* Correspondence, remarkably curious, is still * extant. The Religion of the times drove them at length to finish their days in two separate Convents. When ABELARD died (which happened about the year 1134), his Body was carried to HELOISA, who buried it in the Convent of the *Paraclete*, where she presided.

MY Countryman, JOHN OF SALISBURY,

* An octavo Edition of their Letters in *Latin* was published at *London*, in the year 1718.

P. III. comes next, who lived in the reign of *Stephen*, and *Henry the Second*. He appears to have been converſant in *all the Latin Claſſics*, whom he not only quotes, but appears to underſtand, to reliſh, and to admire *.

How far they ſunk into his Mind, and inſpired him with ſentiments ſimilar to rheir own, the following paſſages may ſuffice to ſhew.

TAKE his Ideas of LIBERTY and SERVITUDE.

" *For, as the true and only* LIBERTY *is* " *to ſerve Virtue, and diſcharge its various* " *duties; ſo the only true and eſſential* SLAVERY *is to be in ſubjection to the Vices.* " *He therefore is evidently miſtaken, who* " *imagines that either of theſe Conditions*

* See *Philoſophical Arrangements*, p. 457.

" *can*

"*can proceed from any other Cause: for*
"*indeed (if we except the difference of*
"VIRTUE *and* VICE) *all men throughout*
"*the world proceed from a similar begin-*
"*ning; consist of, and are nourished by the*
"*same elements; draw from the same prin-*
"*ciple the same vital breath; enjoy the same*
"*cope of heaven; all alike live; all alike*
"*die**.

TAKE his idea concerning the extensive influence of PHILOSOPHY.

"'*Tis* PHILOSOPHY, *that prescribes a*
"*just measure to all things; and while she*

* *Sicut enim vera et unica* LIBERTAS *est, servire virtuti, et ipsius exercere officia; ita unica et singularis* SERVITUS *est vitiis subjugari. Errat plane quisquis aliunde conditionem alterutram opinatur accidere. Si quidem omne hominum genus in terris simili ab ortu surgit, eisdem constat et alitur elementis, eundemque spiritum ab eodem principio carpit, eodemque fruitur cælo, æque moritur, æque vivit.* De Nugis Curialium, p. 510. Edit. Lugdun. 1595.

P. III. "*arranges moral Duties, condescends to* "*mix with sueh as are plebeian and* "*vulgar.—No otherwise, indeed, can any* "*thing be said to proceed rightly, unless* "*she herself confirm by* DEEDS, *what* "*she teaches us in* WORDS *.

Speaking of VIRTUE and FELICITY, he thus explains himself.—

"*But these* (two possessions) *are more* "*excellent than any other, because* VIRTUE *includes all things, that are to be* "*done*; FELICITY, *all things that are* "*to be wished. Yet does* FELICITY *excel* "VIRTUE, *because in all things the End* "*is more excellent than the Means. Now*

* *Ipsa* (PHILOSOPHIA) *est, quæ universis præscribit modum, et dum disponit officia, etiam plebeis, et vulgaribus interesse dignatur. Alioquin nihil aliud recte procedit, nisi et ipsa rebus afferat, quod verbis docet.* De Nugis Curial. p. 483.

"*no*

"*no one is* HAPPY, *that he may act* Ch. X.
"rightly; *but he acts* RIGHTLY, *that he*
"*may live* happily *."

THE following Diſtich is of his own Age, but being difficult to tranſlate, is only given in its original, as a ſample of elegant and meritorious Poetry.

IT expreſſes a *refined* thought; that *as the Soul of Man animates the Body, ſo is the Soul itſelf animated by God.*

Vita Animæ DEUS *eſt; hæc, Corporis; hac fugiente,*
Solvitur hoc; perit hæc, deſtituente Deo †.

---

* *Sunt autem hæc omnibus aliis præſtantiora, quia* VIRTUS *omnia agenda,* FELICITAS *omnia optanda complectitur. Felicitas tamen Virtuti præſtat, quia in omnibus præſtantius eſt propter quod aliquid, quam quod propter aliquid. Non enim felix eſt quis, ut recte agat; ſed recte agit, ut feliciter vivat.* De Nugis Curial. p. 367, 368.

† Ibid. p. 127.

P. III. THE preceding Quotations are taken from his Tract *De Nugis Curialium:* those, which follow, are from another Tract called METALOGICUS, so named from being subsequent to *Logic,* as METAPHYSICS are to *Physics.*

HE makes *three* things requisite to the existence of every ART, and these are GENIUS, MEMORY, and THE REASONING FACULTY, and these *three* he thus *defines*—

" GENIUS *is a certain Power, naturally* " *implanted in the Mind, and which is* " *of itself* ORIGINALLY CAPABLE *.

" MEMORY *is (as it were)* THE " MIND'S ARK *or* CHEST; *the firm*

* *Est autem* INGENIUM *vis quædam, animæ naturaliter insita, per se valens.* Metalog. p. 756.

"*and faithful preserver of things per-*
"*ceived* *.

"THE REASONING FACULTY *is a* "*power of the Mind, which examines* "*things, that have occured either to* THE "SENSES, *or to* THE INTELLECT, *and* "*fairly decides in favour of the better*; "*which, well weighing the* SIMILITUDES "*and* DISSIMILITUDES *of things, at* "*length (after due discussion) establishes* "ART, *and shews it to be (as it were)* "A FINITE SCIENCE OF THINGS IN-"FINITE †."

OUR

---

* MEMORIA *vero quasi* MENTIS ARCA, *firma et fidelis custodia perceptorum.* Metalog. p. 757.

† RATIO *eorum, quæ Sensibus aut animo occurrunt, examinatrix animi vis est, et fidelis arbitra potiorum; quæ, rerum similitudines dissimilitudinesque perpendens, tandem* ARTEM *statuit quasi quandam* INFINITORUM FINITAM ESSE SCIENTIAM. Metalog. 757.

P. III.

Our Author concludes with telling us, that "*As* Nature *is the* Mother *of all* "Arts, *so the Contempt of them surely* "*redounds to the Injury of their* Pa-"rent *."

This may be illustrated from *the Arts* of Arithmetic and Grammar.

Numbers, which are infinite, being reduced to the finite Genera of *Even* and *Odd*; and these again being divided into the few subordinate Species: in this *limited Reduction* we behold the Rise of Arithmetic, and of all the various Theorems contained in that Art.

Sounds Articulate, which are infinite, being reduced to the finite Genera of *Vowels* and *Consonants*; and *Vowels* again being enlarged into the species of *Long*, *Short*, and *Middle*; *Consonants* into the Species of *Mutes* and *Liquids*: in these *limited Reductions* we behold the Rise of Grammar; thro' which, by about twenty *Simple Sounds* called *Letters*, we form *Articulate Sounds* by Millions.

* *Quia* Artium Natura *mater est, merito in injuriam parentis redundat contemptus earum.* Metalog. 757.

I must

I MUST not omit some of his *Grammatical* ideas, because they are of a superior sort, that is to say, they are *Logical* and *Philosophical*.

He tells us—*For as* [IN NATURE] ACCIDENTS *cloath* SUBSTANCES, *and give them a* FORM; *so* [IN LANGUAGE] *through a similar correspondence are* SUBSTANTIVES *vested with a* FORM *by* ADJECTIVES. *And that this* [grammatical] *Institution of* REASON *may the more easily coincide with* NATURE; *in the same manner as the* SUBSTANCE OF EVERY NATURAL BEING *knows nothing of* INTENSION *and* REMISSION; *so likewise in* LANGUAGE SUBSTANTIVES *admit no* DEGREE OF COMPARISON *.

* *Sicut enim* ACCIDENTIA SUBSTANTIAM *vestiunt, et informant: sic quadâm proportione* RATIONIS *ab* ADJECTIVIS SUBSTANTIVA informantur. *Et, ut familiarius* RATIONIS *Institutio* NATURÆ *cohæreat, sicut* SUBSTANTIA *cujusque rei* INTENTIONIS *et* REMISSIONIS *ignara est:* sic SUBSTANTIVA *ad* COMPARATIONIS GRADUM *non veniunt.* Metalog. 561.

AFTER

P. III.

AFTER this he proceeds to ſhow that *this Imitation of Nature* not only exiſts in *Nouns*, but in *the other Parts of Speech*. He tells us, that VERBS, as they denote TIME, are neceſſarily provided with TENSES; and, as they always expreſs *ſomething elſe* in their *original meaning*, he calls the *additional denoting of Time* by a truly *philoſophic* Word, a CONSIGNIFICATION *.

THE writer of theſe Remarks cannot ſay he has transferred any of them into his *Hermes*, becauſe *Hermes* was written long before he knew *John of Saliſbury*. But, that both Writers drew from the ſame ſource, he thinks ſufficiently clear from the ſimilitude of their ſentiments †.

* MOTUS *non eſt ſine* TEMPORE, *nec* VERBUM *eſſe potuit ſine* TEMPORIS CONSIGNIFICATIONE. Metalog. 561. *Ariſtot. de Interpret. c.* 3.

† See *Hermes*, p. 95, 96, 97.

I FEAR,

Ch. X.

I FEAR, I have dwelt too long on my *Countryman*, perhaps, becauſe a countryman; but more in truth, becauſe his Works are little known, and yet are certainly curious and valuable.

I SHALL only mention, that there were other reſpectable Geniuſes of *the ſame Century*, ſuch as the *Epic Poet*, JOSEPH OF EXETER; *the pleaſant Archdeacon of Oxford*, WALTER MAPPS; GIRALDUS CAMBRENSIS, &c.

BUT the eloquent *Author of the Life of Henry the Second* has in his third Volume handled the ſtate of our Literature *during this period* in ſo maſterly a way, that the writer of theſe obſervations would not have ſaid ſo much, had not the Arrangement of his Remarks made it in ſome degree neceſſary *.

---

* See Lord Lyttelton's Life of Henry the Second.

P. III.

We muſt not conclude this Chapter without relating a few Facts, relative to the gallant Richard, called from his *Magnanimity Cœur de Leon*. Other *Heroes*, long before him, had been likened to *Lions*; and the celebrated *Ali*, in the lofty language of *Arabia*, was called *the Lion of God*.

What *Bohadin* ſays of Richard is remarkable. " He was, as that Hiſtorian " relates, uncommonly active; of great " ſpirit and firm Reſolution; one, who " had been ſignalized by his Battles, " and who was of intrepid courage " in War. By thoſe, whom he led, " he was eſteemed *leſs than the King of* " *France* on account of his Kingdom, " and Dignity, but more abundant in " Riches, and *far more illuſtrious for mi-* " *litary Valour* *."

* *Bahadin, vit. Salad.* p. 160.

This

THIS Teſtimony receives no ſmall weight, as it comes from a *contemporary* writer, who was *preſent*; and who, being likewiſe a faſt Friend to *Saladin*, *Richard*'s great Antagoniſt, can hardly be ſuſpected of flattering *an Adverſary*. Ch. X

IN the following Extracts from the ſame Author, which Extracts contain *Different* Conferences between *Richard* and *Saladin*, we have a ſample of their *ſentiments*, and of *the manner* in which they *expreſt* them.

WHEN RICHARD in *Paleſtine* was ill, he longed for Fruit and Ice, and the fruits he deſired were Pears and Peaches. He ſent for them to *Saladin*, and they were immediately given him. *Richard* in return was equally bountiful, and entertained the Sultan's people magnificently. War between great men ſeldom extinguiſhes Humanity *.

* *Bahadin*, p. 176.

AFTER

P. III. AFTER a long and various War, RICHARD sent to SALADIN the following MESSAGE.

"WHEN you have greeted the Prince, "you will lay what follows before him— "The *Musselmans* and *Francs* are both "perishing; their countries laid waste, "and completely passing to ruin; the "wealth and Lives of their people con- "sumed on either side. To this Contest "and *Religious War* its proper Rights have "been now paid. Nothing remains to "be settled, but the affair of *the Holy City*, "of *the Cross*, and of *the several Regions* "or Countries. As to *the Holy City*, it "being the seat of our Worship, from *that* "indeed we can by no means recede, "altho' not a single man of us were to "survive the attempt. As to *the Coun-* "*tries*, those on this side *Jordan*, shall "be restored to us. As to *the Cross*, it "being *with you* only a pitiful piece of "Wood, altho' *to us* of value inestimable,

"This

"This *the Sultan* will give us; and thus "Peace being eſtabliſhed, we ſhall all of "us reſt from this our uninterrupted fa-"tigue *.

SALADIN'S ANSWER TO RICHARD.

"THE HOLY CITY is as much holy "to *us*, as to *you*; nay, is rather of "greater worth and dignity *to us*, than *to* "*you*; as 'twas *thence* that *our Prophet* "took his Journey by night to Heaven; "'tis *there the Angels* are wont ſolemnly "to aſſemble themſelves. Imagine not "therefore that we ſhall ever depart "thence. We dare not among *the Muſ-* "*ſulmans* appear ſo abandoned, ſo neg-"lectful of our Affairs, as to think of "this. As to THE REGIONS or COUN-"TRIES, theſe alſo you know were ori-"ginally ours, which you indeed have

* *Bohaden*, p. 207.

"an-

P. III. "annexed to your Dominions by the "Imbecillity of *the Muſſulmans* at the "period, when you attacked them. God "has not ſuffered you to lay a ſingle ſtone "there, ever ſince the War began; while "we, 'tis evident, enjoy all the produce "of our Countries to the full. Laſtly, "as to the Cross, that in truth is *your* "Scandal, and a great diſhonour to the "Deity; which, however, it does not be-"come us, by giving up, to neglect, un-"leſs it be for ſome more important ad-"vantage, accruing thence to the Faith of "*Mahomet* *."

It muſt be obſerved, that *the Croſs* here mentioned was ſuppoſed to have been that, on which *Chriſt* was crucified; and which being in *Jeruſalem*, when it was taken, had been from that time in the hands of *Saladin*.

* *Bohadin*, p. 208.

THO' no Peace was now made, it was made ſoon after, yet without reſtoration either of *Jeruſalem*, or of *the Croſs*. Ch. X.

'TWAS uſual in thoſe days to ſwear to Treaties, and ſo did the inferior Parties; but the *two Monarchs* excuſed themſelves, ſaying, *it was not uſual for Kings to ſwear* *."

WHEN RICHARD was returning home, he was baſely ſeized by *a Duke of Auſtria*, and kept priſoner for more than a year, till by a large ſum raiſed upon his people he was redeemed †.

THIS gallant Prince, after having eſcaped for years the moſt formidable perils,

---

* *Bohadin*, p. 261.

† See the Hiſtories of *Richard's* Life, *Rapin*, *Hume*, &c.

P. III. fell at length unfortunately by the Arrow of an obſcure hand, in beſieging an obſcure Caſtle, within *his own French* Domains.

He did not immediately die; but, as the wound began to mortify, and his end to approach, he ordered the perſon, who had ſhot him (his name was *Bertramn de Gurdun)* to be brought into his preſence.

When he arrived, the King thus addreſt him. "*What harm have I ever done* "*thee? for what reaſon haſt thou ſlain* "*me?*" *Bertramn* replied—"*Thou haſt* "*ſlain my Father and two Brothers with* "*thy own hand; and now 'twas thy deſire* "*to ſlay* ME. *Take then any Vengeance* "*upon me thou wilt; I ſhall freely ſuffer* "*the greateſt tortures thou canſt invent, ſo* "*that* THOU *art but diſpatched, who haſt* "*done the world ſo much miſchief.*"

The

THE King, on this intrepid anſwer, commanded his Chains to be taken off; forgave what he had done, and diſmiſt him with a Preſent. Ch. X.

BUT the King's ſervants were not ſo generous, as their maſter; for, when the King was dead, (which ſoon happened) they put the priſoner to a cruel death.

A POET of the time compares, not improperly, the Death of RICHARD to that of a *Lion*, killed by an *Ant*. The *ſentiment* is better than the *Metre*.

Iſtius in morte perimit Formica Leonem *.

'TIS

* *Rogeri de Heredon Annalium pars poſterior*. p 791, Edit. Francof. 1601. We have tranſcribed from the original the Diſcourſe, which paſt between *Richard* and *Bertramn*, as it appears to be curious, and the *Latinity* not to be deſpiſed.

Quid mali tibi feci? Quare me interemiſti?—Cui ille reſpondit—*Tu interemiſti patrem meum, et duos fratres*

 manu

P. III. 'Tis ſomewhat ſingular, that in theſe Periods, conſidered as dark and barbarous, *the ſame Nations* ſhould ſtill retain their *ſuperiority of Taſte*, tho' not perhaps in its original purity. During the reign of *Henry the Third*, (which ſoon followed) when Biſhop *Poore* erected *the Cathedral of Saliſbury* (which conſidering its lightneſs, its uniformity, and the height of its Spire, is one of the completeſt *Gothic* buildings now extant) we are informed he ſent into Italy for the beſt Architects *.

Long before this, in the eighth Century, when one of the *Caliphs* erected a moſt *magnificent Temple or Moſque* at *Damaſcus*,

manu tuâ, et ME *nunc interimere voluiſti. Sume ergo de me vindictam, quamcunque volueris: libenter enim* patiar, *quæcunque excogitaveris majora tormenta, dummodo* TU *interficiaris, qui tot et tanta mala contuliſti mundo.*

* *Matthew Paris.*

he procured for the builing of it the moſt ſkilfull Architects, and thoſe not only from his own Dominions, but (as the Hiſtorian informs us) from GREECE *.

FROM theſe accounts it is evident, that ſome Knowlege of the FINE ARTS, even during this *middle Age*, exiſted both in ITALY and GREECE.

SHOULD it be demanded, *to which Nation, in this reſpect, we give the Preference*,—it is a Queſtion to be decided by recurring to Facts.

ITALY at the beginning of her Hiſtory was barbarous; nor did ſhe emerge from her Barbarity, till GREECE, which ſhe had conquered, gave her Poets, Orators, Philoſophers, &c.

---

* *Abulfed.* p. 125.

P. III.

GRÆCIA captu ferum VICTOREM cepit —— HOR.

AFTER a ſucceſſion of Centuries the *Roman Empire* fell. By this fatal Event the *Finer Arts* fell alſo, and lay for years in a kind of torpid ſtate, till they revived through the genial warmth of GREECE.

A FEW GREEK Painters, in the *thirteenth* Century, came from *Greece* into *Italy*, and taught their Art to CIMABUE, a *Florentine* *. *Cimabue* was the Father of *Italian Painters*, and from him came a Succeſſion, which at length gave the *Raphaels*, the *Michael Angelo's*, &c.

THE *Statues*, and ruined *Edifices*, with which *Italy* abounded, and which were all of them by GREEK Artiſts, or after GRE-

* *Cimabue died in* 1300.

CIAN Models, taught the *Italians* the Fine *Arts* of *Sculpture* and *Architecture* *. Ch. X.

THE GREEK FUGITIVES from *Constantinople*, after it's unhappy Cataſtrophe, brought that ſuperior *Literature* into *Italy*, which enabled the *Italians* to read in the original the capital Authors of ATTIC ELOQUENCE †.

WHEN *Literature*, *Sculpture*, *Architecture*, and *Painting* had thus attained a perfection in *Italy*, we learn from Hiſtory, they were tranſplanted into *the North*, where they lived, tho' it was rather like *Exotics*, than *Natives*.

As therefore *Northern Europe* derived them from *Italy*, and *this laſt* from

* *How early* theſe fine Remains began to excite their admiration, we learn from thoſe warm Verſes of *Hildebert*, quoted before, p. 427.

† Sup. p. 319.

P. III. *Greece,* the conclusion is evident, that NOT ITALY, but GREECE WAS THEIR COMMON PARENT. And thus is the Question concerning *Preference* to be decided.

CHAP.

CHAP. XI.

Concerning the POETRY *of the* LATTER LATINS, *or* WESTERN EUROPEANS—*Accentual Quantity*—RHIME—*Samples of* RHIME *in Latin—in Claſſical Poets, accidental; in thoſe of a later age, deſigned*—RHIME *among the Arabians*—ODILO, HUCBALDUS, HILDIGRIM, HALABALDUS, *Poets or Heroes of Weſtern Europe*—RHIMES *in* MODERN *Languages—of Dante, Petrarch, Boccaccio, Chaucer, &c.—Sannazarius, a pure Writer in Claſic Latin, without Rhime—Anagrams, Chronograms, &c. finely and accurately deſcribed by the ingenious Author of the* SCRIBLERIAD.

AND here, as we are about to ſpeak upon the POETRY of theſe times; we wiſh our Readers previouſly to review, what we have already ſaid upon the *two* Ch.XI.

P. III. *Species of verbal Quantity*, the *Syllabic* and the *Accentual* *.

It will there appear that till *Greek* and *Latin* degenerated, *Accentual* Quantity was hardly known. But tho' *Degeneracy* ſpred it thro' theſe two Languages, yet, with regard to *modern* Languages, 'twas the beſt that could be attained. Their harſh and rugged *Dialects* were in *few* inſtances ſuited to the *Harmonious Simplicity* of the *Syllabic Meaſure*.

And yet, tho' this more perfect and elegant *Proſody* was rarely attainable, ſo ſtrong was the Love of Mankind for Rhythm, ſo *connate* (if I may ſo ſay) with their very Being, that Metre *of ſome*

* See from p. 74 to p. 92.

ſort was every where cultivated, and even these *northern* Tribes had their *Bards*, their *Minſtrels*, their *Troubadours*, and the like. Ch. XI.

Now, tho' in THE LATTER LATINITY *Syllabic Quantity* was little regarded, and the *Accentual* more frequently ſupplied it's place, they did not eſteem even *this laſt* always ſufficient *to mark the Meaſure*. An Expedient was therefore found (flattering to the Ear, becauſe it had ſomething of *Harmony*) and this was, *to mark the laſt Syllables* of different Verſes with *Sounds that were Similar*, ſo that the Ear might not doubt a moment, where every Verſe *ended*.

AND hence in *Modern* Verſe *theſe laſt Syllables*, which Poets of *a purer* Age in a manner *neglected*, came to claim a peculiar and *ſuperior* regard, as helping to mark the RHYTHM thro' the medium of the RHIME.

Si

P. III.

*Si Sol ſpendeſcat Mariâ purifi*CANTE,
Major erit glacies poſt feſtum, quam fuit ANTE *.

NOR was this practiſed in *Heroics only*, but in *Trochaics* alſo.—

Suſcitavit igitur || *Deus Hebræ*ORUM
Chriſtianos principes, || *et robur* EORUM
Vindicare ſcilicet || *Sanguinem Sanct*ORUM,
Subvenire filiis || *Mortifica*TORUM †.

NAY ſo fond were thoſe Poets of their Jingle, that they not only infuſed it into *different* Verſes, but into *one and the ſame*

* RHIME *is the* SIMILITUDE OF SOUND *at the Ends of two Verſes.* RHYTHM *is* MEASURED MOTION, *and exiſts in Verſes of every ſort, whether Claſſical or not Claſſical, whether Blank Verſe, or Rhime.* In ſhort, WITHOUT RHYTHM *no Verſe can exiſt of any ſpecies*; WITHOUT RHIME *they may, and often do.*

† *Roger Hoveden. Annal* p. 379, b.

Verſe;

Verſe; making *the Middle* of each Verſe to rhime with *its End,* as well *as one Verſe* to rhime with *another.* Ch. XI.

Thus in *St. Edmund's* Epitaph we read—

Hic erat EDMUNDUS, *animâ cum corpore* MUNDUS,
Quem non IMMUNDUS *potuit pervertere* MUNDUS *.

And again in thoſe verſes tranſcribed from an old monument——

*Hic ſunt con*FOSSA *Bernoldi præſulis* OSSA;
Laudet cum GLOSSA, *dedit hic quia munera* GROSSA.

To theſe may be added the Inſcription upon the three Wiſe Men of the Eaſt, buried (as they tell us) at *Cologn* in the Weſt.

---

* *Waverly*, p. 202.

Corpora

P. III.

*Corpora sanc*TORUM *recubant hic terna Ma*-
GORUM,
*Ex his sub*LATUM *nihil est, alibive lo*-
CATUM.

VERSES of this sort, of which there are innumerable still extant, have been called *Leonine* Verses, from *Leo*, a writer of the 12th Century, who is supposed to have been their inventor. But this should seem a mistake, if the Inscription upon the Image of a King *Dagobert*, who lived in *the seventh* Century, be of the same period with that Monarch.

Fingitur hac specie, bonitatis odore REFER-
TUS,
Istius Ecclesiæ fundator, Rex DAGOBERTUS.

'TIS true there are Verses of this sort to be found even among Poets, *the first in classical rank*.

Thus VIRGIL,

Trajicit: i, VERBIS *virtutem illude su*PERBIS.

Thus

Thus HORACE,

*Fratrem mæ*RENTIS, *rapto de frātre* DOLENTIS.

Thus even HOMER himſelf,

'Εκ γὰρ κρηΤΑΩΝ γένος ἔυχομαι ἐυρειΑΩΝ.

THE difference ſeems to have been, THE RHIMES, falling from theſe *ſuperior* Geniuſes, fell ('twas probable) *accidentally:* with the *latter* race of Poets they were the Work of *labour* and *deſign*. They may well indeed be called Works *of labour and deſign*, when we reflect on the immenſe pains, which their makers muſt have taken, where *their Plan of Rhiming* was ſo *complicated*, as they ſometimes made it.

TAKE a ſingular example of no fewer than *three* RHIMES to each Verſe.

Crimina CRESCERE *flete*; TEPESCERE *jus, decus*, ÆQUUM;
Flete, GEMISCITE; *denique* DICITE, *dicite* MECUM,

P. III.

Qui regis OMNIA, *pelle tot* IMPIA, *surge*, PERIMUS,
Nos, Deus, ASPICE, *ne sine* SIMPLICE *lamine* SIMUS.

Fabricius, who gives these Verses, remarks, that they were written in the *Dactylic Leonine*; that is, they had every Foot *a Dactyl*, excepting the last, and contained *three Rhimes* in each Verse, TWO *within the Verse* itself, and ONE *referring to the Verse that followed.* He adds, that their Author, *Bernardus Morlanensis*, a Monk of the eleventh Century, composed no less than *three* Books of this wonderful Versification. What leisure must he have had, and how was it employed *?

BEFORE we quit the subject of RHIME we may add, that RHIME was used not only by the *Latin*, but by the *Arabian*

* See *Fabric. Biblioth. med. et infim. ætatis*, under the word, *Bernardus Morlanensis*.

Poets,

Poets, as we may ſee by a tract upon the *Arabic* Proſody, ſubjoined by Dr. *Pococke* to his *Carmen Tograï*. Ch. XI.

Rhime however was not ſo ſtrictly followed, but that ſometimes they quitted it. In the following *Heroics*, the Monk *Odilo*, addreſſing himſelf to his Friend *Hucbaldus*, appears ſo warm in his wiſhes, as not only to forget *Rhime*, but even *Claſſical* Quantity.

Hucbaldo Sōpho Sōphīă sĭt semper amica;
Hucbaldus Sōphus Sōphīæ semper amicus:
Expóſco hoc Odĭlo, peccator cernuus ēgo.

This Genius (over whoſe Verſes I have occaſionally marked the *accentual* Quantity in contra-diſtinction to the *Syllabic*) is ſuppoſed to have written in the *tenth* Century.

Others, *rejecting Rhime*, wrote *Elegiacs*; as that Monk, who celebrated

 Hildĭ-

P. III. *Hildīgrim* and *Halabuldus*; the one for building a Church, the other for consecrating it.

Hildīgrim ſtruxīt; Hălăbaldus Epiſcopus
Archi
Sanctificavit: honor certus utrumque
manet.

IN the firſt of theſe two Verſes the word *Archi-Epiſcopus* is, by a pleaſant *tranſpoſition*, made into a *Dactyl* and *Spondree*, ſo as to complete the Hexameter *.

'TWAS upon *theſe* Principles of Verſification, that the early Poets of this Æra wrote much bad *Verſe* in much bad *Latin*. At length they tried their ſkill in their *Vernacular* tongues, introducing *here* alſo their *Rhime* and their *Accen-*

* See *Recueil de divers Ecrits pour ſervir de l' Eclairciſſements a l' Hiſtoire de France* par *L' Àbbe de Beuf*, p. 115.—p. 106.

tual

tual quantity, as they had done before in *Latin*. Ch. XI

THRO' the Southern parts of *France* the TROUBADOURS (already mentioned) * composed Sonnets in the *Provençal* Tongue. Soon after them DANTE, PETRACH, and BOCCACCIO wrote Poems in *Italian*; and soon after these, CHAUCER flourished in *England*. From *Chaucer*, thro' *Rowley*, we pass to Lords *Surry* and *Dorset*; from them to *Spencer*, *Shakspeare*, and *Johnson*: after whom came *Milton*, *Waller*, *Dryden*, *Pope*, and a succession of Geniuses, down to the present time.

THE THREE ITALIAN POETS, we have mentioned, were capital in their kind, being not only strong and powerful in *Sentiment*, but, what is more surprising, elegant in their *Diction* at a time, when

* See before, p. 411.

P. III. *the Languages of England* and *France* were barbarous and unpolished. This in *English* is evident from our Countryman, CHAUCER, who, even to an *English* Reader appears so uncouth, and who yet wrote later than the latest of these three.

IT must, however, be acknowleged, that, if *we except his Language*, for LEARNING and WIT he appears equal to the best of his *Contemporaries*, and I may add even of his *Successors*.

I CANNOT omit the following *sample of his* LITERATURE, in the *Frankelein's Tale*. In that Poem the fair *Dorigen* is made to lament the absence of her much loved *Arveragus*; and, as she sits upon a Cliff, beholding the Sea, and the formidable Rocks, she breaks forth with terror into the following Exclamation.

Eternal GOD! *that thro' thy Purveyaunce*
LEADEST *the World by* CERTAIN *Governaunce*;

IN

IN IDLE, *as men ſayn,* YE NOTHING MAKE.
But, Lord, thoſe grieſly, fendly, ROCKIS, *blake,*
That ſeem rathir a FOUL CONFU'SIÓN
Of Work, than any FAIR CREA'TIÓN
OF SUCH A PERFECT GOD, *wiſe, and full ſtable*:
WHY *have ye wrought this work unréaſonáble?*

Dorigen, after more expoſtulation of the ſame ſort, adds—

I wote well Clerkis woll ſayn, as 'hem leſte,
By Arguments, that ALL IS FOR THE BESTE,
Tho' I ne cannot well the Cauſes know—
But thilké God, that made the Winds to blow,
Ay keep my Lord, &c.

THERE is an elegant Pathos in her thus quitting thoſe deeper Speculations, to ad-

P. III. dreſs a Prayer for the ſafety of her *Arveragus.*

The Verſe, before quoted,

To LEAD *the World by* CERTAIN *Governaunce,*

is not only a *philoſophical Idea,* but *philoſophically* expreſt.

The next Verſe,

IN IDLE, *as Men ſayn,* YE NOTHING MAKE,

is a ſentiment tranſlated literally from ARISTOTLE, and which that Philoſopher ſo much approved, as *often* to repeat it.

TAKE one Example—

Ὁ δὲ Θεὸς καὶ ἡ φύσις, οὐδὲν μάτην ποιοῦσιν— GOD *and* NATURE MAKE NOTHING IN VAIN. *Ariſt. de Cælo, Lib.* I. *Cap.* 4.

As to what follows, *I mean that ſpeculation of learned men, that* ALL IS FOR THE BEST, this too we meet in *the ſame* Philo-

Philosophy, annexed (as it were) to *the* Ch. XI.
sentiment just alleged.

Η φύσις ὖθεν δημιουργεῖ μάτην, ὥσπερ εἴρηται πρότερον, ἀλλὰ πάντα πρὸς τὸ Βελτιον ἐκ τῶν ἐνδεχομένων. NATURE, *(as has been said before)* CREATES NOTHING IN VAIN, *but* ALL THINGS FOR THE BEST, *out of the contingent materials. De Animal. incessu. C.* 12.

IT may be fairly doubted, whether CHAUCER took this from the *original Greek*—'tis more probable he took it from the *Latin Version* of the *Spanish Arabic Version*, which *Latin* was then current, and admitted thro' *Western Europe* for the *Aristotelic Text*.

The same thought occurs in one of our most elegant *modern* Ballads; tho', whence the Poet took it, I pretend not to decide.

P. III. *How can they ſay, that* NATURE
HAS NOTHING MADE IN VAIN?
Why then beneath the Water
Do HIDEOUS ROCKS *remain?*
THOSE ROCKS *no eyes diſcover,*
Which lurk beneath the deep,
To wreck, &c.

BUT to return to CHAUCER—

IF in *the Tale* we have juſt quoted; if in the Tale of the *Nun's Prieſt*, and in many other of his works, there are theſe ſprinklings of *Philoſophy*; if to theſe we add the extenſive Knowlege of *Hiſtory*, *Mythology*, and various other ſubjects, which he every where ſhews: we may fairly, I think, arrange him among our *learned* Poets, and take from HIM *an Eſtimate of the Literature of the Times*, as far at leaſt as poſſeſt by men of *ſuperior* Education.

AFTER having mentioned (as we have lately done) PETRARCH and ſome of the *Italians*,

Italians, I can by no means omit their countryman SANNAZARIUS, who flouriſhed in the Century following, and whoſe Eclogues in particular, formed on the Plan of *Fiſhing* Life inſtead of *Paſtoral*, cannot be enough admired both for their *Latinity* and their *Sentiment*. His fourth *Eclogue*, called *Proteus*, written in imitation of *Virgil's* Eclogue called *Silenus*, may be juſtly valued as a maſter-piece in its kind. The following ſlight ſketch of it is ſubmitted to the Reader. Ch.XI.

" Two Fiſhermen, ſailing during a
" dark night from *Caprea* into the Bay of
" Naples, as they ſilently approach the
" Promontory of *Minerva*, hear PROTEUS
" from the Shore, ſinging a marvelous
" Narrative of the ſtrange Events, of
" which *thoſe Regions* had been the well-
" known Scene. He concludes with the
" unhappy fate of the Poet's Friend and
" Patron, *Frederic King of Naples*, who,
" having

P. III. "having been expelled his Kingdom, "died an Exile in *France.*"

If I might be pardoned a digreſſion, it ſhould be on the Elegance of the *Numbers*, by which this unfortunate part of the Tale is introduced.

Addit triſtia fata, et te, quem luget ademptum
Italia, &c.

The Omiſſion of the *uſual Cæſura*, in the firſt of theſe verſes, naturally throws it into that *Anapæſtic Rhythm*, ſo finely ſuited to *ſolemn* Subjects.

Addit—triſtia—fata et—te quem, &c. *

It may be obſerved alſo, in how *pathetic*, and yet withal, in how *manly* a way *Sannazarius* concludes. *Frederic* died in a remote region, and was buried, where he

* So *Homer*,

Πότνια—θέα μή—μόι τόδε—χώεο.

Odyſſ. E. 215.

he died. "*'Tis pleasing*, says PROTEUS, "*for a man's remains to rest in his own* "*Country; and yet for a Tomb every Land* "*suffices.*"

Grata quies patriæ, sed et omnis terra Sepulcrum.

THOSE, who know how much sooner *Italy* emerged from Barbarity, than the rest of *Europe*, may chuse to place SANNAZARIUS rather at the *beginning* of a *good* age, than at the *conclusion* of a *bad* one. Their opinion, perhaps, is not without foundation, and may be extended to FRACASTORIUS, POLITIAN, POGGIUS, and many other eloquent Authors, which that Century then produced, when Eloquence was little known elsewhere.

BEFORE we quit *Poetry*, we shall say something upon its *lowest* Species, upon *Acrostics*, *Chronograms*, *Wings*, *Altars*, *Eggs*, *Axes*, &c.

P. III.

THESE were the poor Inventions of men *devoid of Taſte*, and yet abſurdly aiming at Fame by theſe deſpicable whims. Quitting the paths of Simplicity and Truth (of which 'tis probable they were wholly ignorant) they aſpired, like Rope-dancers, to Merit, which only lay in *the difficulty*. *The Wings*, the *Axes*, the *Altars*, &c. were *wretched Forms*, into which they tortured poor *Words*, juſt as poor *Trees* in our Gardens were formerly mangled into Giants, Flower-Pots, Pea-cocks, Obeliſcs, &c.

WHOEVER remembers that ACROSTICS, in Verſification, are formed from the *Initial Letter* of every Verſe, will ſee the Force and Ingenuity of the following deſcription.

Firm and compact, in three fair Colums wove,
O're the ſmooth plain the bold ACROSTICS *move:*

HIGH

HIGH *o're the reſt* THE TOW'RING LEADERS RISE,
With LIMBS GIGANTIC *and* SUPERIOR SIZE.

CHRONOGRAMS, by a different conceit, *were not confined to* INITIAL LETTERS, but, as they were *to deſcribe Dates*, THE NUMERAL LETTERS, *in whatever part of the Word they ſtood*, were diſtinguiſhed from *other* Letters *by being written in* CAPITALS.

FOR example, I would mark by a CHRONOGRAM the Date 1506. I take for the purpoſe the following Words,

—feriam ſidera vertice;

and by *a ſtrange Elevation of* CAPITALS I compel even *Horace* to give me *the Date required.*

—feriaM ſiDera VertIce, MDVI.

THE Ingenious Author, whom I have quoted before, thus admirably deſcribes this *ſecond* ſpecies of folly.

Not

P. III.

Not thus the looser CHRONOGRAMS *prepare;*
Careless their Troops, undisciplin'd to War;
With RANK IRREGULAR, CONFUS'D *they stand,*
THE CHIEFTAINS MINGLING *with the vulgar band.*

IF I have dwelt too long on these trifles, it is not so much for their *merit* (of which they have none) as for those *elegant* Lines, in which they are so well described.

ON the same motive I conclude this Chapter with selecting a few more Lines from the same ingenious Poem.

To join these squadrons, o'er the champain came
A numerous race, of no ignoble name;
RIDDLE, *and* REBUS, *Riddle's dearest Son,*
And false CONUNDRUM, *and insidious* PUN;

FUSTIAN,

Fustian, *who ſcarcely deigns to tread the ground,*
And Rondeau, *wheeling in repeated round.*
On their fair ſtandards, by the winds diſplay'd;
Eggs, Altars, Wings, Pipes, Axes *were pourtray'd* *.

---

* See the Scribleriad, (Book II. V. 151, &c.) of my valuable Friend, Mr. *Cambridge* of *Twickenham*.

CHAP. XII.

PAUL *the Venetian,* *and* SIR JOHN MANDEVILLE, *great Travellers* — SIR JOHN FORTESCUE, *a great Lawyer* — *his valuable Book, addreſt to his Pupil, the Prince of Wales* — KING'S COLLEGE CHAPEL *in Cambridge,* FOUNDED BY HENRY THE SIXTH.—

'TWAS during this middle Period lived thoſe celebrated Travellers, PAUL THE VENETIAN, and our Countryman, SIR JOHN MANDEVILLE.

WE have mentioned CHAUCER before them, tho' he flouriſhed *after both*; for *Chaucer* lived till paſt the year 1400, PAUL began his Travels in the year 1272, and MAUDEVILLE began his in the year 1322. The Reaſon is, *Chaucer* has been arranged with *the Poets, already* ſpoken of.

MARC

MARC PAUL, who is the firſt Writer of any Note concerning the *Eaſtern* Countries, travelled into thoſe remote Regions as far as the Capital and Court of *Cublai Chan*, the ſixth from that tremendous Conqueror *Jingiz Chan**. *Paul* is a curious and minute Relator of what he ſaw there. C. XII.

He deſcribes *the Capital*, CAMBALU, to be a ſquare walled in, of *Six miles* on every ſide, having to each ſide three Gates, and the ſeveral ſtreets rectilinear, and croſſing at right angles.

The Imperial Palace, he tells us, was incloſed within a ſquare wall of *a mile* on every ſide, and was magnificently adorned with Gilding and Pictures. 'Twas a piece of ſtate, that thro' the grand or principal gate no one could enter but the Emperor *himſelf*.

WITHIN the walls of this Square there

* See *Abulpharajius*, from p. 281 to p. 306.

P. III. were extenſive Lawns, adorned with Trees, and ſtockt with wild animals, ſtags, goats, fallow deer, &c. not to mention a River, which formed a Lake, filled with the fineſt fiſh.

Besides this, at a League's diſtance from the Palace, he deſcribes a ſmall Mountain or Hill, planted with Ever-greens, in circumference about a mile. "Here (he tells us) the Emperor had all "the fineſt trees that could be procured, "brought to him, employing his Ele-"phants for that purpoſe, as the trees "were extracted with their roots.

"The Mountain, from its verdure, "was called the Green Mountain. "On its ſummit ſtood a fine Palace, diſ-"tinguiſhed alſo by its *Green* Colour, "where he *(the Great Chan)* often retired "to enjoy himſelf *."

Speak-

* The preceding Extracts are taken from a *Latin* Edition of Paulus Venetus, publiſhed, in a ſmall Quarto,

SPEAKING of *the Person* of *Cublai*, the then Monarch, he thus describes him. C.XII.

"HE is remarkably handsome; of a "moderate stature; neither too corpulent, "nor too lean; having a Countenance "ruddy and fair; large eyes; a beautiful "Nose; and all the lineaments of his "Body formed in due proportion *."

Quarto, *Coloniæ Brandenburgicæ, ex officina Georgii Schulzii anno* 1679.

As the Book is not rare, nor the stile curious, we have only given the several Pages, by way of reference.

For *the Capital*, CAMBALU, see p. 68. *Lib.* 2. *Cap.* 10.

For *the Imperial Palace, Lawns* adjoining, and *the Green Mountain*, see p. 66, 67, *Lib.* 2. *Cap.* 9.

* *Rex* CUBLAI *est homo admodum pulcher, staturâ mediocri, non nimis pinguis, nec nimis macilentus, faciem habens rubicundam atque candidam, oculos magnos, nasum pulchrum, et omnia corporis lineamenta debitâ proportione consistantia.* Mar. Pauli Lib. 2. Cap. 8. p. 65.

P. III. WE here quit our Traveller, only observing, as we conclude, that learned men have imagined this CAMBALU to be PEKIN in *China*, founded there by *Jingiz Chan*, soon after he had conquered it.

WHEN we consider the immense Power of this mighty Conqueror, who in a manner subdued the vast Tract of *Asia*; we are *the less difficult* in believing such marvellous Relations. The City, the Palace, and the Territory around teach us, what was the *Taste* of him and his Family, whose boundless Empire could admit of *nothing minute*.

IT is too an additional argument for *Credibility*, that, tho' the Whole is *Vast*, yet nothing appears either *Foolish*, or *Impossible*.

ONE thing is worthy of notice, that, tho' PAUL resided in *China* so long, he makes no mention of the *celebrated* WALL.

WALL.—Was this *forgetfulneſs* ? or was it not *then* erected ? C. XII.

As to our Countryman, SIR JOHN MANDEVILLE, tho' he did not travel ſo far as *Marc Paul*, he travelled into many Parts of *Aſia* and *Africa*; and, after having lived in thoſe Countries for thirty-three years, died at *Liege* in the year 1371.

HE wrote his Travels in three Languages, *Latin*, *French*, and *Engliſh*, from the laſt of which Languages we quote, taking the liberty, in a few inſtances, to modernize the *Words*, tho' not in the minuteſt degree to change the *Meaning*.

WE confine ourſelves for brevity to a ſingle fact.

TRAVELLING thro' *Macedonia*, he tells us, as follows—" In this Country was " ARISTOTLE born, in a City, that men

P. III. "call *Strageris* *, a little from the City "of *Tragie* or *Trakys*; and at *Strageris* "is *Aristotle* buried, and there is an Altar "at his Tomb, where they make a great "Feast every Year, as tho' he was a Saint. "Upon this Altar the Lords (or Rulers) "hold their Great Councils and Assemblies, for they hope, that, thro' the inspiration of God and of Him, they shall "have the better counsel †."

Such was the Veneration (for it was more than Honour) paid by the *Stagirites* to their Countryman, more than *eighteen hundred years* after his death ‡.

---

* Its antient name in *Greek* was Στάγειρα, whence *Aristotle* was often called, by way of eminence, The Stagirite, as being a Citizen there.

† See *Mandeville's* Voyages, Chap. 2.

‡ Those, who desire a taste of this great Man's Philosophy in *English*, may find their curiosity amply gratified in the last work of that learned and acute *Grecian*, Lord Monboddo, which work he stiles Antient Metaphysics, published in Quarto at *Edinburgh*, 1779.

From

FROM theſe times we paſs over the triumphant reign of *Henry the Fifth* (a reign rather of *Action* than of *Letters)* to that of his unfortunate Son. This was a Period, diſgraced by unſucceſsful wars abroad, and by ſanguinary diſorders at home. *The King himſelf* met an *untimely* End, and ſo did his hopeful and high ſpirited *Son*, the *Prince of Wales.* Yet did not even theſe Times keep one Genius from emerging, tho' plunged by his rank into their moſt tempeſtuous part. By this I mean SIR JOHN FORTESCUE, Chancellor of *England*, and Tutor to *the young Prince*, juſt mentioned. As this laſt office was a Truſt of the greateſt importance, ſo he diſcharged it not only with conſummate *Wiſdom*, but (what was more) with conſummate *Virtue*. C. XII.

HIS Tract IN PRAISE OF THE LAWS OF ENGLAND *, is written with the nobleſt

* This Book, which he ſtiles DE LAUDIBUS LEGUM ANGLIÆ, is written in Dialogue between himſelf,

P. III. bleſt view that man ever wrote; written to inſpire his Pupil with a Love of the Country he was to govern, by ſhewing him that, TO GOVERN BY THOSE ADMIRABLE LAWS, would make him a FAR GREATER PRINCE, than the moſt UNLIMITED DESPOTISM *.

THIS he does not only prove by a detail of *particular Laws*, but by an accurate

---

ſelf, and the young Prince his Pupil, and was originally in *Latin*. The great *Selden* thought it worthy of a Commentary, and ſince that it has been publiſhed and enriched with additional Notes by Mr. *Gregor*. A new Edition was given ann. 1775, and the Latin Text ſubjoined.

* See of *Forteſcue*'s Work, Chap. IX. and XIII. and, above all, Chap. XIV. where he tells us *the Poſſibility of doing amiſs*, (which is the only Privilege an *abſolute* Prince enjoys above a *limited* one) *can be called* AN ADDITION OF POWER *no other, than we ſo call* A POSSIBILITY TO DECAY, OR TO DIE. See p. 41 of the Engliſh Verſion.

'Tis worth obſerving that *Forteſcue*, in his dialogue, gives theſe fine ſentiments to the *young Prince*, after he has heard much and due Reaſoning upon the excellence of our Conſtitution. See Chap. XXXIV. p. 119.

com-

comparison between the state of *England* and *France*, one of which he makes a Land of *Liberty*, the other of *Servitude*. His thirty-fifth and thirty-sixth Chapters upon this subject are invaluable, and should be read by every ENGLISHMAN, *who honours that* NAME. C. XII.

THRO' these and the other Chapters, we perceive an *interesting Truth*, which is, that the capital parts of our Constitution, the *Trial by Juries*, the *Abhorrence of Tortures*, the *Sovereignty of Parliament* as well in the granting of *Money*, as in the making and repealing of *Laws*, I say, that all these, and many other inestimable privileges, existed THEN, as they do NOW; were not *new* projects of the Day, but SACRED FORMS, to which *Ages* had given a venerable *Sanction* *.

As

* For trial by *Juries*, see of this *Author* Chap. XX, XXI, and XXII.—For his abhorrence of *Torture*, see

P. III. As for the LITERATURE of this Great Man (which is more immediately to our purpose) he appears to have been a Reader of *Aristotle*, *Diodorus Siculus*, *Cicero*, *Quinctilian*, *Seneca*, *Vegetius*, *Boethius*, and many other ancients; to have been not un-informed in the Authors and History of *later* Ages; to have been deeply knowing not only in *the Laws of his own Country* (where he attained the highest dignity they could bestow) but in *the Roman* or *Civil Law*, which he holds to be far inferior *; we must add to this a masterly insight into the *State* and *Policy* of the *neighbouring Nations*.

PERHAPS

see Chap. XXIII —For the *sovereignty of Parliament* see Chap IX, XIII, XVIII, XXXVI, particularly p. 118 of the *English Version*.—For the high antiquity of our *Laws* and *Constitution*, see Chap. XVII.

* The inferiority of the *Roman* Law to *our own*, is a Doctrine he strongly inculcates. See above all Chap. IX, XIX, &c. also Chap. XXXIV, where he nobly reprobates, as he had done before in Chap. IX, that infamous

PERHAPS a perſon of Rank, *even at preſent*, need not wiſh to be better inſtituted, if he had an ambition to ſoar above the Faſhionable Poliſh. C.XII.

WE muſt not conclude, without obſerving that the Taſte for *Gothic Architecture* ſeems never to have been ſo *elegant*, as during this period; witneſs that exquiſite ſtructure, built by *Henry the Sixth*, I mean THE CHAPEL OF KING'S COLLEGE in *Cambridge*.

---

infamous maxim, *Quod* PRINCIPI *placuit*, LEGIS *habet Vigorem*, a Maxim, well becoming an *Oriental Caliph*, but hardly decent even in a *degenerate Roman Law-giver*.

CHAP.

CHAP. XIII.

Concerning NATURAL BEAUTY — *its Idea the ſame in all Times* — THESSALIAN TEMPE — *Taſte of* VIRGIL, *and* HORACE — *of* MILTON, *in deſcribing Paradiſe* — *exhibited of late years firſt in Pictures* — *thence transferred to* ENGLISH *Gardens* — *not wanting to the enlightened Few of the middle Age* — *proved in* LELAND, PETRARCH, *and* SANNAZARIUS, — *compariſon between the Younger* CYRUS, *and* PHILIP LE BEL *of France.*

BUT let us paſs for a moment from the elegant Works of ART to the more elegant Works of NATURE. The two ſubjects are ſo *nearly* allied, that *the ſame Taſte* uſually reliſhes them *both.*

Now there is nothing more certain, than that the Face of *inanimate Nature* has been at all times captivating. *The Vulgar,* indeed, look no farther than to Scenes of *Culture,*

Culture, because all their Views merely terminate in *Utility*. They only remark, that 'tis fine Barley; that 'tis rich Clover; as an Ox or an Ass, if they could speak, would inform us. But *the Liberal* have *nobler* views, and tho' they give to *Culture* is due Praise, they can be delighted with *natural Beauties*, where *Culture* was *never* known. C.XII.

Ages ago they have celebrated with enthusiastic rapture "*a deep retired Vale,* "*with a River rushing thro' it; a Vale* "*having it's sides formed by two immense* "*and opposite Mountains, and those sides* "*diversified by Woods, Precipices, Rocks* "*and romantic Caverns.*" Such was the Scene, produced by the River *Penēus*, as it ran between the Mountains, *Olympus* and *Ossa*, in that well known Vale, the Thessalian Tempe*.

Virgil

---

* *Est nemus Hæmoniæ, prærupta quod undique claudit Silva: vocant* Tempe. *Per quæ Peneus ab imo*

Effusus

P. III. VIRGIL and HORACE, the firſt for Taſte among the *Romans*, appear to have been enamoured with Beauties of this character. HORACE prayed for a Villa, where there was *a Garden*, a *Rivulet*, and above theſe *a little Grove*.

Hortus ubi, et tectò vicinus jugis aquæ fons,
Et paulùm Silvæ ſuper his foret.
Sat. VI. 2.

VIRGIL wiſhed to enjoy *Rivers*, and *Woods*, and to be hid under immenſe ſhade in the cool *valleys* of Mount *Hæmus*—

—O! qui me gelidis in Vallibus Hæmi
Siſtat, et ingenti ramorum protegat umbra?
Georg. II. 486.

Effuſus Pindo ſpumoſis volvitur undis,
Dejectuque gravi, &c.
Ovid. Metam. Lib. I. 568.

A fuller and more ample account of this beautiful ſpot may be found in the *Firſt Chapter* of the *Third Book of Ælian's Various Hiſtory*.

THE

THE great ELEMENTS of *this* ſpecies of Beauty, according to *theſe* Principles, were WATER, WOOD, and UNEVEN GROUND; to which may be added a fourth, that is to ſay, LAWN. 'Tis the happy *Mixture* of theſe four, that produces every Scene of *natural Beauty*, as 'tis a more myſterious Mixture of *other* Elements (perhaps as *ſimple*, and *not more* in number) that produces a *World* or *Univerſe*. C.XIII.

Virgil and *Horace* having been quoted, we may quote, with equal truth, our great countryman, MILTON. Speaking of the Flowers of *Paradiſe*, he calls them *Flowers*,

——*which* NOT NICE ART
In beds and curious Knots, but NATURE BOON
Pours forth profuſe on hill, and dale, and plain.

P. L. IV. 245.

SOON

P. III.

Soon after this he ſubjoins—

—— *this was the Place*
A happy rural Seat, of VARIOUS VIEW.

He explains this Variety, by recounting the Lawns, the Flocks, the Hillocks, the Valleys, the Grotts, the Waterfalls, the Lakes, &c. &c. and in another Book, deſcribing the approach of *Raphäel,* he informs us, that this divine Meſſenger paſt

—— *Thro' Groves of Myrrh,*
And flow'ring Odors, Caſſia, Nard and Balm,
A Wilderness *of Sweets; for Nature here*
Wanton'd as in her prime, and play'd AT WILL
Her Virgin-fancys, pouring forth more ſweet,
Wild ABOVE Rule *or Art,* ENORMOUS Bliss.—

P. L. IV. 292.

The

THE *Painters* in the preceding Century feem to have felt the power of thefe *Elements*, and to have transferred them into their Landfcapes with fuch amazing force, that they appear not fo much to have *followed*, as to have *emulated* Nature. *Claude de Lorraine, the Pouffins, Salvator Rofa*, and a few more, may be called *fuperior Artifts* in this exquifite Tafte. C.XIII.

Our Gardens in the mean time were taftelefs and infipid. Thofe, who made them, thought *the farther they wandered from Nature*, the nearer they approached *the Sublime*. Unfortunately, where they travelled, *no Sublime was to be found*; and the farther they went, the farther they left it behind.

BUT *Perfection*, alas! was not the work of a day. Many Prejudices were to be removed; many gradual Afcents to be made; Afcents from Bad to Good, and from Good to Better, before the *deli-*

P. III. *cious Amenities* of a *Claude* or a *Poussin* could be rivalled in a *Stour-head*, a *Hagley*, or a *Stow*; or *the tremendous Charms* of a *Salvator Rosa* be equalled in the Scenes of a *Peircefield*, or a *Mount Edgecumb*.

NOT however to forget the subject of our Inquiry.—Tho' 'twas not before the *present* Century, that we established a chaster Taste; tho' our neighbours at this instant are but learning it from us; and tho' to the Vulgar every where it is totally incomprehensible (be they Vulgar in rank, or Vulgar in capacity): yet, even in the darkest periods we have been treating, periods, when Taste is often thought to have been lost, we shall still discover *an enlightened few*, who were by no means insensible to the power of *these* beauties.

How warmly does LELAND describe *Guy's Cliff*; SANNAZARIUS, his Villa of *Mergilline*; and PETRARCH, his favourite *Vaucluse*?

TAKE

TAKE GUY's CLIFF from *Leland* in his own *old English*, mixt with *Latin*— "*It is a place meet for the Muses; there* "*is Sylence; a praty wood; antra in vivo* "*saxo*; (Grottos in the living Rock) *the* "*River roling over the stones with a praty* "*noyse.*" His *Latin* is more elegant— *Nemusculum ibidem opacum, fontes liquidi et gemmei, prata florida, antra muscosa, rivi levis et per saxa decursus, nec non solitudo et quies Musis amicissima**. C.XIII.

MERGILLINE, the Villa of *Sannazarius* near *Naples*, is thus sketched in different parts of his Poems.

Exciso in scopulo, fluctus unde aurea canos
Despiciens, celso se culmine MERGILLINE
Attollit, nautisque procul venientibus offert.
Sannaz. De partu Virgin. I. 25.

---

* See *Leland's Itinerary*, Vol. IV. p. 66.

P. III.

Rupis O! ſacræ, pelagique cuſtos,
Villa, Nympharum cuſtos et propinquæ
Doridos——
Tu mihi ſolos nemorum receſſus
Das, et hærentes per opaca lauros
Saxa: Tu, fontes, Aganippedumque
Antra recludis.

Ejuſd. Epigr. I. 2.

——*quæque in primis mihi grata miniſtrat*
Otia, Muſarumque cavas per ſaxa latebras,
MERGILLINA; *novos fundunt ubi citria flores,*
Citria, Medorum ſacros referentia lucos.

Ejuſd. De partu Virgin. III. ſub fin.

De Fonte Mergillino.

Eſt mihi rivo vitreus perenni
Fons, arenoſum prope littus, unde
Sæpe deſcendens ſibi nauta rores
Haurit amicos, &c.

Ejuſd. Epigr. II. 36.

'TWOULD

'TWOULD be difficult to tranſlate theſe elegant Morſels.—'Tis ſufficient to expreſs what they mean, *collectively*—"that the "Villa of MERGILLINA had ſolitary "WOODS; had GROVES of Laurel and "Citron; had GROTTOS in the Rock, "with RIVULETS and SPRINGS; and "that from ITS LOFTY SITUATION it "lookt down upon the Sea, and com-"manded an extenſive proſpect." C.XIII.

'TIS no wonder that *ſuch a Villa* ſhould enamour *ſuch an Owner*. So ſtrong was his affection for it, that, when during the ſubſequent Wars in *Italy*, it was demoliſhed by the Imperial Troops, this unfortunate Event was ſuppoſed to have haſtened his end*.

---

* So we learn from *Paulus Jovius*, the writer of his Life, publiſhed with his Poems by *Græviuſ*, in a ſmall Edition of ſome of the *Italian* Poets, at *Amſterdam*, in the year 1695.

P. III. * VAUCLUSE (*Vallis Clausa*) the favourite retreat of PETRARCH, was a romantic Scene, not far from *Avignon*.

" It is a VALLEY, having on each " hand, as you enter, immense Cliffs, " but *closed up* at one of its Ends by a " semi-circular Ridge of them; from " which *incident* it derives *its name*. One " of the most stupendous of these Cliffs " stands in the front of the semi-circle, " and has at its foot an opening into an " immense *Cavern*. Within the most *re-* " *tired and gloomy part* of this Cavern is " a *large oval Bason*, the production of " Nature, filled with pellucid and un- " fathomable Water; and from this re- " servoir issues a River of respectable " magnitude, dividing, as it runs, the " Meadows beneath, and winding thro' the " Precipices, that impend from above *."

* See *Memoires pour la Vie de François Petrarque*, Quarto, Tom. I. p. 231, 341, 342. See also *Plin. Nat. Hist*, L. XXVIII. c. 22,

THIS

THIS is an imperfect ſketch of that ſpot, where PETRARCH ſpent his time with ſo much delight, as to ſay that *this alone* was Life to him, the reſt but a ſtate of puniſhment. C.XIII.

IN the two preceding Narratives I ſeem to ſee an anticipation of that Taſte for *natural* Beauty, which now appears to flouriſh thro' *Great Britain* in ſuch perfection. It is not to be doubted that the *Owner of Mergillina* would have been charmed with *Mount Edgecumb*; and *the Owner of Vaucluſe* have been delighted with *Pierceſield.*

WHEN we read in XENOPHON*, that the *younger* CYRUS had with his own hand planted *trees for Beauty,* we are not ſurpriſed, tho' pleaſed with the Story,

* See the *Oeconomics of Xenophon,* where this Fact is related.

P. III. as *the Age* was *polished*, and *Cyrus* an accomplished Prince. But, when we read that in the beginning of the 14th Century, *a King of France* (PHILIP LE BELL) should make it penal to cut down a Tree, *qui a este gardè pour sa beaultè, which had been preserved* FOR ITS BEAUTY; tho' we praise the Law, we cannot help being surprised, that the Prince should at such a period have been so far enlightened*.

---

* See a valuable Work, intitled *Observations on the Statutes, chiefly on the antient*, &c. p. 7, by the Honble. Mr. *Barrington*; a work, concerning which it is difficult to decide, whether it be more entertaining, or more instructive.

CHAP.

CHAP. XIV.

SUPERIOR LITERATURE *and* KNOWLEGE *both of the Greek and Latin* CLERGY, *whence*—BARBARITY *and* IGNORANCE *of the* LAITY, *whence—Samples of Lay-manners, in a Story from* ANNA COMNENA'*s Hiſtory*—CHURCH AUTHORITY *ingeniouſly employed to check Barbarity—the ſame Authority employed for other good purpoſes—to ſave the poor Jews—to ſtop Trials by Battle—more ſuggeſted concerning Lay-manners—Ferocity of the* NORTHERN LAYMEN, *whence—different Cauſes aſſigned*—INVENTIONS *during the dark Ages—great, tho' the Inventors often unknown—Inference ariſing from theſe Inventions.*

BEFORE I quit the LATINS, I ſhall ſubjoin two or three Obſervations on THE EUROPEANS in general. Chap. XIV.

THE

P. III. THE *superior* Characters for *Literature* here enumerated, whether in the *Western* or *Eastern Christendom* (for 'tis of *Christendom only* we are now speaking) were by far the greater part of them ECCLESIASTICS.

IN this number we have selected from among THE GREEKS *the Patriarch of Constantinople*, PHOTIUS; MICHAEL PSELLUS; EUSTATHIUS and EUSTRATIUS, *both of Episcopal Dignity*; PLANUDES; *Cardinal* BESSARIO—from among THE LATINS, *Venerable* BEDE; GERBERTUS, afterwards POPE SYLVESTER THE SECOND; INGULPHUS, *Abbot of Croyland*; HILDEBERT, *Archbishop of Tours*; PETER ABELARD; JOHN OF SALISBURY, *Bishop of Chartres*; ROGER BACON; FRANCIS PETRARCH; *many Monkish Historians*; ÆNEAS SYLVIUS, afterwards POPE PIUS THE SECOND, &c.

SOME-

Chap. XIV.

SOMETHING has been already ſaid concerning each of *theſe*, and other *Eccleſiaſtics**. At preſent we ſhall only remark, that 'twas neceſſary, *from their very Profeſſion*, that they ſhould *read* and *write*; accompliſhments, at that time *uſually confined to themſelves*.

THOSE of the *Weſtern* Church were obliged to acquire ſome knowlege of LATIN; and for GREEK, to thoſe of the *Eaſtern* Church it was ſtill (with a few Corruptions) their *native* Language.

IF we add to theſe Preparations *their mode of Life*, which, being attended moſtly with a decent competence, gave them immenſe leiſure; 'twas not wonderful that,

* Thoſe, who wiſh to ſee more particulars concerning theſe learned Men, may recur to their Names in the Index, or, if he pleaſe, may conſult the *Third* Part of theſe Inquiries, in Chapters IV. IX. X. XI. XIV.

among

P. III. *among such a multitude, the more meritorious* should emerge, and soar by dint of Genius above the common herd. Similar Effects proceed from similar Causes. The Learning of *Egypt* was possest by their *Priests*; who were likewise left from their institution to a life of leisure*.

For the Laity on the other side, who, from their mean Education, wanted all these Requisites, they were in fact no better than what *Dryden* calls them, *a tribe of Issachar*; a race, from their cradle bred in *Barbarity*, and *Ignorance*.

A Sample of these illustrious *Laymen* may be found in Anna Comnena's History of her Father *Alexius*, who was

---

* *Aristotle*, speaking of *Egypt*, informs us — ἐκεῖ γὰρ ἠφείθη σχολάζειν τὸ τῶν ἱερέων ἔθνος — *For there* (meaning in *Egypt*) THE TRIBE OF PRIESTS *were left* TO LEAD A LIFE OF LEISURE. *Arist. Metaph.* L. I. c. 1.

Grecian

Grecian Emperor in the *eleventh* Century, when the first CRUSADE arrived at *Constantinople*. So promiſcuous a Rout of rude Adventurers could not fail of giving umbrage to the *Byzantine Court*, which was ſtately and ceremonious, and conſcious withal of its internal debility. Chap. XIV.

AFTER ſome altercation, the Court permitted them to paſs into *Aſia* thro' the *Imperial* Territories, upon their *Leaders* taking *an Oath of Fealty* to the Emperor.

WHAT happened at the performance of this Ceremonial, is thus related by the fair Hiſtorian above mentioned.

" ALL the Commanders being aſ-
" ſembled, and GODFREY OF BULLOIGN
" himſelf among the reſt, as ſoon as the
" Oath was finiſhed, one of the *Counts*
" had the audaciouſneſs to ſeat himſelf
" *beſide the Emperor* upon his throne.

" *Ear*

P. III. "*Earl Baldwin*, one of *their own* people, "approaching, took *the Count* by the "hand; made him riſe from the throne; "and rebuked him for his inſolence.

"The *Count* roſe, but made no reply, "except it was in his own unknown "Jargon to mutter abuſe upon the Em-"peror.

"When all things were diſpatched, "the *Emperor* ſent for this man, and "demanded, *who he was, whence he came,* "*and of what Lineage?*—His anſwer "was as follows—*I am a genuine* Frank, "*and in the number of their Nobility.* "*One thing I know, which is, that in a* "*certain part of the Country I came from,* "*and in a place, where three ways meet,* "*there ſtands an antient Church, where* "*every one, who has a deſire to engage in* "*ſingle Combat, having put himſelf into* "*fighting order, comes and there implores*

"*the*

Chap. XIV.

" *the assistance of the Deity, and then*
" *waits in expectation of some one, that*
" *will dare attack him. On this spot* I
" MYSELF *waited a long time, expecting*
" *and seeking some one, that would arrive,*
" *and fight me. But* THE MAN, THAT
" WOULD DARE THIS, *was no where to*
" *be found**.

---

* Those, who attend to *this* Story, and who have perused any of the Histories of *Chivalry*, in particular an ingenious *French* Treatise upon the subject, in two small Volumes 8vo. published at *Paris*, in the year 1759, intitled, *Mémoires sur l'ancienne Chevalerie*, will perceive that the much admired *Don Quixote* is not an *Imaginary Character*, but a Character, drawn after the *real Manners* of the times. 'Tis true indeed, the Character is somewhat *heightened*; but even *here* the witty Author has contrived to make it *probable*, by ingeniously adding a certain mixture of *Insanity*.

These *Romantic Heroes* were not wholly extinct even in periods *far later* than *the Crusades*. THE CHEVALIER BAYARD flourished under *Francis the First of France*, and LORD HERBERT OF CHERBURY under *James* and *Charles the First of England*.

" THE

P. III.

" THE *Emperor*, having heard this " strange Narrative, replied pleasantly— " *If at the time, when you sought War,* " *you could not find it, a Season is now* " *coming, in which you will find Wars* " *enough. I therefore give you this ad-* " *vice: not to place yourself either in the* " *Rear of the Army, or in the Front,* " *but to keep among those, who support the* " *Centre; for I have long had knowlege* " *of the Turkish method in their Wars*.*"

THIS was one of those COUNTS, or BARONS, *the petty Tyrants of Western Europe*; men, who, when they were not engaged in *general* wars, (such as the ravaging of a neighbouring Kingdom, the massacring of Infidels, Heretics, &c.) had no other method of filling up their

* See *Anna Comnena's* History of her Father, *Fol. Gr. Lat.* p. 300.

leisure,

leiſure, than, thro' help of their *Vaſſals*, by waging war upon one another. Chap. XIV.

AND here the *Humanity* and *Wiſdom* of THE CHURCH cannot enough be *admired*, when by *her authority* (which was then mighty) ſhe endeavoured to *ſhorten* that ſcene of Bloodſhed, which ſhe could not *totally* prohibit. THE TRUCE OF GOD (a name given it *purpoſely* to render the meaſure more *ſolemn)* enjoined *theſe ferocious Beings*, under the terrors of *Excommunication*, not to fight *from Wedneſday Evening to Monday Morning*, out of reverence to the *Myſteries*, accompliſhed on the other four days; the *Aſcenſion* on Thurſday; the *Crucifixion* on Friday; the *Deſcent to Hell* on Saturday; and the *Reſurrection* on Sunday*.

I hope

* See any of the Church Hiſtories of the time, in particular an ingenious French Book, entitled *Hiſtoire Eccleſiaſtique*, in two Volumes, 12mo. digeſted into *Annals*,

P. III.

I hope a farther obſervation will be pardoned, when I add that *the ſame Humanity* prevailed during the fourteenth Century, and that *the terrors of* CHURCH POWER were then held forth with an intent *equally* laudable. A dreadful plague at that period deſolated all *Europe*. *The Germans*, with no better reaſon than their own *ſenſeleſs Superſtition*, imputed this calamity to *the Jews*, who then lived among them in great opulence and ſplendour. Many thouſands of theſe unhappy people were inhumanly maſſacred, till *the Pope* benevolently interfered, and prohibited by the ſevereſt Bulls ſo mad and ſanguinary a proceeding *.

Annals, and having the ſeveral years marked in the courſe of the Narrative. Go to the years 1027, 1031, 1041, 1068, 1080.

* See the *Church Hiſtories* about the middle of the fourteenth Century, and *Petrarch's Life*.

I could

I could not omit *two* ſuch *ſalutary* exertions of *Church Power*, as they both occur within the period of this Inquiry. I might add *a third*, I mean the oppoſing and endeavouring to check that abſurdeſt of all Practices, THE TRIAL BY BATTLE, which *Spelman* expreſsly tells us that THE CHURCH in all ages *condemned**.

Chap. XIV.

IT muſt be confeſſed, that the Fact juſt related concerning the *unmannered* Count, at the Court of *Conſtantinople*, is rather againſt the order of *Chronology*, for it happened during the firſt Cruſades. It ſerves however to ſhew *the Manners* of the *Latin* or *Weſtern Laity*, in the beginning of *that Holy War*. They did not, in a ſucceſſion of years, grow *better*, but *worſe*.

---

* *Truculentum morem in omni ævo acriter inſectarunt* THEOLOGI, &c. See before, p. 243.

P. III. 'TWAS a Century after, that another Crusade, in their march against Infidels, sacked this very City; deposed the then Emperor; and committed Devastations, which no one would have committed, but the most ignorant, as well as cruel Barbarians. If we descend not at present to particulars, it is, because we have already quoted so largely from Nicetas, in a former Chapter *.

BUT a Question here occurs, easier to propose, than to answer.—" To what are " we to attribute this character of FEROCITY, which seems to have then pre-" vailed thro' THE LAITY OF EUROPE?

* See Part III. chap. 5, and Abulpharagius, p. 282, who describes their indiscriminate Cruelty in a manner much resembling that of their Brother Crusaders at Bezieres, and that nearly about the same time. See before, p. 409.

SHALL

Shall we say, 'twas Climate, and the Nature of the Country?—These we must confess have in some instances great Influence.

The Indians, seen a few years since by Mr. *Byron* in the southern parts of *South America*, were brutal and savage to an enormous excess. One of them, for a trivial offence, murdered his own Child (an infant) by dashing it against the Rocks. *The Cyclopes*, as described by *Homer*, were much of the same sort; each of them gave Law to *his own* Family, without *regard for one another*; and besides this, they were *Atheists* and *Man-eaters*.

May we not suppose, that a stormy sea, together with a frozen, barren, and inhospitable shore might work on the Imagination of these *Indians*, so, as by banishing all *pleasing* and *benign* Ideas, to fill

P. III. them with *habitual* Gloom, and a Propensity to be cruel?—or might not the *tremendous* Scenes of *Etna* have had a like Effect upon the *Cyclopes*, who lived amid Smoke, Thunderings, Eruptions of Fire, and Earthquakes? If we may believe *Fazelius*, who wrote upon *Sicily* about two hundred years ago, the *Inhabitants* near *Etna* were in *his* time a similar Race *.

If therefore these *limited* Regions had such an effect upon their *Natives*, may not a similar Effect be presumed from *the vast Regions of the North?* May not its cold, barren, uncomfortable *Climate* have made its numerous Tribes *equally rude* and *savage?*

If this be not enough, we may add *another* Cause, I mean their *profound Igno-*

* See *Fazelius de Rebus feculis*, L. II. c. 4.

rance,

rance. Nothing mends THE MIND more than CULTURE, to which these Emigrants had no desire, either from Example or Education, to lend a patient Ear.

Chap. XIV.

WE may add *a farther Cause still*, which is, that, when they had acquired Countries better than their own, they *settled* under *the same Military Form*, thro' which they had *conquered*; and were in fact, when settled, *a sort of Army after a Campaign*, *quartered* upon the wretched remains of *the antient Inhabitants*, by whom they were attended under the different names of *Serfs*, *Vassals*, *Villains*, &c.

'TWAS not likely the Ferocity of these *Conquerors* should abate with regard to their *Vassals*, whom, as strangers, they were more likely to suspect, than to love.

P. III. 'Twas not likely it ſhould abate with regard to one another, when the *Neighbourhood* of their Caſtles, and the *Contiguity* of their Territories, muſt have given occaſions (as we learn from Hiſtory) for endleſs Altercation. But this we leave to the learned in Feudal Tenures.

We ſhall add to the preceding Remarks one more ſomewhat *ſingular*, and yet perfectly *different*; which is, that tho' the Darkneſs in *Weſtern Europe*, during the Period here mentioned, was (in Scripture Language) *a Darkneſs that might be felt*, yet is it ſurpriſing that, during a Period ſo obſcure, many *admirable Inventions* found their way into the world; I mean ſuch as *Clocks*, *Teleſcopes*, *Paper*, *Gunpowder*, *the Mariner's Needle*, *Printing*, and a number here omitted *.

---

* See two ingenious Writers on this Subject, *Polydore Virgil*, *De Rerum Inventoribus*; and *Pancirollus*, *De Rebus perditis et inventis*.

'Tis

'Tis surprising too, if we consider the *importance* of these arts, and their *extensive utility*, that it should be either *unknown*, or *at least doubtful, by whom* they were *invented*. Chap. XIV.

A lively Fancy might almost imagine, that every Art, as it was wanted, had suddenly started forth, addressing those that sought it, as *Eneas* did his companions —

—*Coram, quem quæritis, adsum.*

Virg.

And yet, Fancy apart, of this we may be assured, that, tho' *the particular Inventors* may unfortunately be forgotten, the Inventions themselves *are clearly referable to* Man; *to that subtle, and active Principle*, Human Wit, or Ingenuity.

Let me then submit the following Query ——

If

P. III.

If the Human Mind be as truly of *divine* Origin, as every *other* part of the Universe; and if every *other* part of the Universe bear testimony to its *Author:* do not the Inventions above mentioned give us reason to assert, *that* God, in the Operations of Man, never leaves himself without a Witness?

CHAP.

CHAP. XV.

Opinions on PAST *Ages, and the* PRESENT *—Conclusion arising from the Discussion of these Opinions*—CONCLUSION OF THE WHOLE.

AND now having done with THE MIDDLE AGE, we venture to say a word upon THE PRESENT. C. XV.

Every Past Age has in its turn been *a Present Age.* This indeed is obvious, but this is not all; for every *Past* Age, when *present*, has been the object of *Abuse.* Men have been represented by their *Contemporaries* not only as bad, but degenerate; as inferior to their predecessors both in *Morals* and *bodily* Powers.

THIS is an Opinion so generally received, that VIRGIL (in conformity to it) when he would express FORMER times, calls

P. III. calls them ſimply BETTER, as if the Term, *better*, implied *former* of courſe.

> *Hic genus* ANTIQUUM *Teucri, pulcherrima*
> *proles,*
> *Magnanimi Heroes, nati* MELIORIBUS
> *annis.* Æn. vi. 648.

THE ſame opinion is aſcribed by HOMER to old NESTOR, when that venerable Chief ſpeaks of thoſe Heroes, whom he had known in his youth. He relates ſome of their names; *Perithous, Dryas, Cæneus, Theſeus*; and ſome alſo of their exploits; as how they had extirpated the ſavage *Centaurs*—He then ſubjoins

> ——————κέινοισι δ᾽ ἂν ὅτις,
> Τῶν οἳ νῦν βροτοί εἰσιν ἐπιχθόνιοι, μαχέοιτο.
> Ιλ. Α. 271.

> —— *with theſe no one*
> *Of earthly race, as men* ARE NOW, *could*
> *fight.*

As

C. XV.

As theſe Heroes were ſuppoſed to exceed in *ſtrength* thoſe of the *Trojan* War, ſo were the Heroes of *that* period to exceed thoſe, *that came after*. Hence, from the time of the *Trojan* War to that of *Homer*, we learn that *Human Strength* was *decreaſed* by a complete *half*.

Thus the ſame *Homer*,

—— ὁ δὲ χερμάδιον λάϐε χειρὶ
Τυδείδης, μέγα ἔργον, ὃ ȣ̓ δύο γ᾽ ἄνδρε φέροιεν,
Οἷοι νῦν βροτοί εἰσ᾽· ὁ δέ μιν ῥέα πάλλε καὶ οἶος.

Ιλ. Ε. 302.

Then graſp'd Tydides in his hand a ſtone,
A Bulk immenſe, which not TWO MEN *could bear,*
As Men are NOW, *but he* ALONE *with eaſe*
Hurl'd it ——

Virgil goes farther and tells us, that not TWELVE MEN of *his* time (and thoſe too *choſen* ones) could even carry the ſtone, which *Turnus* flung.

Vix

P. III.

Vix illud LECTI BIS SEX *cervice subirent,*
Qualia NUNC *hominum producit corpora tellus:*
Ille manu raptum trepidâ torquebat in hostem. Æn. xii. 899.

THUS *Human* strength, which in HOMER'S TIME was lessened to *half*, in VIRGIL'S TIME was lessened to *a twelfth*. If *Strength* and *Bulk* (as commonly happens) be *proportioned*, what *Pygmies* in *Stature* must the Men of *Virgil's* time have been, when their strength, as he informs us, was so far diminished? A Man *only eight times* as *strong* (and not, according to the Poet, *twelve times*) must at least have been between five and six feet *higher*, than *they* were.

BUT we all know the Privilege, claimed by Poets and Painters.

'Tis in virtue of this Privilege that HORACE, when he mentions the moral Degeneracies of his *Contemporaries*, asserts that " *their Fathers were worse than their*
" *Grand-*

" *Grandfathers; that they were worse than* C. XV.
" *their Fathers; and that their Children*
" *would be worse than they were;*" describing no fewer, after the Grandfather, than *three Successions of Degeneracy*.

> *Ætas parentum*, PEJOR *avis, tulit*
> *Nos* NEQUIORES, *mox daturos*
> *Progeniem* VITIOSIOREM.
>
> Hor. Od. L. iii. 6.

WE need only ask, were this a fact, what would THE ROMANS have been, had they *degenerated in this proportion* for five or six Generations more?

YET JUVENAL, subsequent to all this, supposes a similar *Progression*; a Progression in Vice and Infamy, which was not *complete*, till his own times.

THEN truly we learn, *it could go no farther*.

> *Nil erit* ULTERIUS, *nostris quod moribus addat*

Posteri-

P. III. *Posteritas*, &c.
Omne IN PRÆCIPITI *vitium stetit*, &c.
Sat. i. 147, &c.

BUT even JUVENAL it seems was mistaken, *bad* as we must allow his times to have been. Several Centuries after, without regard to *Juvenal*, the *same* Doctrine was inculcated with greater zeal than ever.

WHEN *the Western Empire* began to decline, and *Europe* and *Africa* were ravaged by *Barbarians*, the Calamities *then* happening (and formidable they were) naturally led Men, who felt them, to esteem *their own Age the worst*.

THE Enemies of *Christianity* (for *Paganism* was not then extinct) absurdly turned these Calamities to the discredit of the *Christian* Religion, and said the times were so unhappy, because the Gods were dishonoured, and the ancient Worship neglected. OROSIUS, a *Christian*, did not deny the melancholy facts, but, to obviate

ate an objection so dishonourable to the true Religion, he endeavours to prove from Historians, both *sacred* and *profane*, that Calamities of *every sort* had existed in *every age*, *as many* and *as great*, as *those* that existed *then*.

C XV.

If Orosius has reasoned right (and his Work is an elaborate one) it follows that the *Lamentations* made *then*, and made ever *since*, are no more than *natural Declamations incidental to Man*; Declamations *naturally* arising, let him live at any period, from *the superior efficacy* of *present Events* upon *present Sensations*.

There is a *Praise belonging to* THE PAST *congenial* with *this Censure*; *a Praise* formed from NEGATIVES, and best illustrated by Examples.

Thus a Declaimer might assert, (supposing he had a wish, by exalting *the eleventh* Century, to debase *the present*)

P. III. that "in the time of THE NORMAN "CONQUEROR we had *no* Routs, *no* Ridot-"tos, *no* Newmarkets, *no* Candidates to "bribe, *no* Voters to be bribed, &c." and ſtring on NEGATIVES, as long as he thought proper.

WHAT then are we to do, when we hear *ſuch Panegyric?* — Are we *to deny* the Facts? — That cannot be — Are we *to admit* the Concluſion? — That appears not quite agreeable. — No method is left but TO COMPARE EVILS WITH EVILS; *the Evils* of 1066 with *thoſe* of 1780; and ſee whether the *former* Age had not *Evils of its own*, ſuch as the *preſent* NEVER *experienced,* becauſe they do *not* NOW *exiſt.*

WE may allow, the Evils of the *preſent* day to be *real* — we may even allow, that a much *larger* number might have been added — but then we may allege evils, by way of return, felt in THOSE *days* ſeverely, but NOW *not* felt at all.

"WE

"We may aſſert, we have not *now*, as C.XV.
"happened *then*, ſeen our Country con-
"quered by foreign Invaders; *nor* our
"Property taken from us, and diſtributed
"among the Conquerors; *nor* ourſelves,
"from Freemen, debaſed into Slaves;
"*nor* our Rights ſubmitted to *unknown*
"Laws, imported, without our conſent,
"from foreign Countries."

Should the ſame Reaſonings be urged in favour of Times, *nearly* as remote, and other Imputations of *Evil* be brought, which, tho' well known *now*, did not *then* exiſt; we may ſtill retort that—"we "are *no longer* NOW, as they were THEN, "ſubject to *feudal* Oppreſſion; *nor* dragged to War, as they were *then*, by the "petty Tyrant of a neighbouring Caſtle; "*nor* involved in ſcenes of blood, as they "were *then*, and that for many years, "during the unintereſting diſputes between A Stephen and A Maud."

P. III.

Should the ſame Declaimer paſs to *a later* period, and praiſe after the ſame manner the reign of Henry the Second, we have then to retort, "*that we* "*have now* no Beckets." Should he proceed to Richard the First, "that *we have now* no Holy Wars"—*to* John Lackland, and his Son, Henry, "that *we have now* no Ba-"rons Wars"—and with regard to both of them, "that, tho' we enjoy at "this inſtant all the benefits of Magna "Charta, we have *not* been compelled "to purchaſe them at the price of our "blood."

A ſeries of Convulſions brings us, in a few years more, to the Wars between the Houſes of York and Lancaster—thence, from the fall of *the Lancaſter Family*, to the calamities of *the York Family*, and its final deſtruction in Richard the Third—thence to the oppreſſive Period

Period of his *avaricious* SUCCESSOR; and from Him to *the formidable* reign of HIS RELENTLESS SON, when *neither* the Coronet, *nor* the Mitre, *nor* even the Crown could protect their wearers; and when (to the amazement of Poſterity) thoſe, by whom *Church Authority* was *denied*, and thoſe, by whom it was *maintained*, were dragged *together to Smithfield*, and burnt *at one and the ſame ſtake* *. C.XV

THE reign of his SUCCESSOR was *ſhort* and *turbid*, and ſoon followed by the *gloomy* one of a BIGOTTED WOMAN.

WE ſtop here, thinking we have inſtances enough. Thoſe, who hear any portion of theſe *paſt* times, *praiſed for the*

* Some of theſe unfortunate men *denied the King's Supremacy*, and others, *the real Preſence*. See the Hiſtories of that Reign.

P. III. *invidious purpose above mentioned*, may anſwer by thus *retorting* the Calamities and Crimes, which *exiſted* AT THE TIME *praiſed*, but which NOW *exiſt no more*. A true Eſtimate can never be formed, but in conſequence of ſuch a *Compariſon*; for if we drop *the laudable*, and allege *only the bad*, or drop *the bad*, and allege *only the laudable*, there is no Age, whatever its real character, but may be made to paſs at pleaſure either for *a good one*, or *a bad one*.

If I may be permitted in this place to add an obſervation, it ſhall be an obſervation founded upon *many* years experience. I have often heard Declamations againſt the *preſent* Race of Men; Declamations againſt them, as if they were *the worſt of animals*; treacherous, falſe, ſelfiſh, envious, oppreſſive, tyrannical, &c. &c. This (I ſay) I have often heard from grave Declaimers, and have heard the Sentiment delivered

delivered with a kind of Oracular Pomp. C. XV. —Yet I never heard any ſuch Declaimer ſay (what would have been *ſincere at leaſt*, if it had been nothing more) "I prove "my aſſertion by an example, where I "cannot err; *I aſſert* MYSELF *to be the* "*Wretch, I have been juſt deſcribing.*"

So far from this, it would be perhaps dangerous to aſk him, even in a gentle whiſper—*You have been talking, with much Confidence, about certain profligate Beings.—Are you certain, that* YOU YOURSELF *are not one of the number?*

I hope I may be pardoned for the following Anecdote, altho' compelled in relating it, to make myſelf a party.

"Sitting once in my Library with a "friend, a worthy but melancholy man, "I read him out of a Book the following "paſſage—

P. III.

"*In our time it may be ſpoken more* "*truly than of old, that Virtue is gone*; "*the Church is under foot*; *the Clergy is in* "*error*; *the Devil reigneth*, &c. &c. My "Friend interrupted me with a ſigh, and "ſaid, *Alas! how true! How juſt a* "*picture of the Times!*—I aſked him, *of* "*what Times?*—*Of what Times*, replied "he with emotion, *can you ſuppoſe any* "*other, but* THE PRESENT? *Were any* "BEFORE *ever ſo bad*, *ſo corrupt*, *ſo* &c.? "—*Forgive me* (ſaid I) *for ſtopping you*— "THE TIMES, *I am reading of*, *are* OLDER "*than you imagine*; *the Sentiment was de-* "*livered above four hundred years ago*; "*its Author* SIR JOHN MANDEVILLE, "*who died in* 1371 *."

* See *this Writer's own Preface*, p. 10, in the large *Octavo English Edition* of his *Travels*, publiſhed at London, in 1727. See alſo of theſe *Philolog. Inquiries*, p. 485.

As

As *Man* is by nature a *social* Animal, GOOD HUMOUR seems an ingredient highly necessary to his character. 'Tis the Salt, which gives a seasoning to the Feast of Life; and which, if it be wanting, surely renders the Feast incomplete. Many Causes contribute to impair this *amiable* Quality, and nothing perhaps more, than *bad Opinions of Mankind*. *Bad Opinions of Mankind* naturally lead us to MISANTHROPY. If these bad opinions go *farther*, and are *applied to the Universe*, then they lead to something worse, for they lead to ATHEISM. The melancholy and morose Character being thus insensibly formed, MORALS and PIETY sink of course; for what EQUALS have we TO LOVE, or what SUPERIOR have we TO REVERE, when we have *no other* objects left, than those of *Hatred*, or of *Terror* *? C. XV.

---

* MISANTHROPY is so dangerous a thing, and goes so far in sapping the very foundations of MORALITY

P. III.

It should seem then expedient if we value our *better* Principles, nay, if we value our own *Happiness*, to withstand such *dreary* Sentiments. 'Twas the advice of a wise Man—*Say not Thou, what is the Cause, that* THE FORMER DAYS WERE BETTER THAN THESE? *For thou*

TY and RELIGION, that I esteem the last part of *Swift's Gulliver* (that I mean relative to his *Hoyhnms* and *Yahoos*) to be a worse Book to peruse, than those which we forbid, as the most flagitious and obscene.

One absurdity in this Author (a wretched Philosopher, tho' a great Wit) is well worth remarking—in order to render *the Nature of* MAN *odious*, and *the Nature of* BEASTS *amiable*, he is compelled to give HUMAN *Characters* to his BEASTS, and BEASTLY *Characters* to his MEN—so that we are to *admire* THE BEASTS, *not for being Beasts*, but *amiable* MEN; and *to detest* THE MEN, *not for being* MEN, *but detestable* BEASTS.

Whoever has been reading this *unnatural* Filth, let him turn for a moment to a *Spectator* of ADDISON, and observe the PHILANTHROPY of that *Classical Writer*; I may add the *superior* Purity of his *Diction* and his *Wit*.

DOST

DOST NOT INQUIRE WISELY *concerning this* *. C. XV.

Things Preſent make Impreſſions amazingly ſuperior to *things Remote*; ſo that, in objects of every kind, we are eaſily miſtaken as to their *comparative* Magnitude. Upon the Canvaſs of *the ſame* Picture *a near* Sparrow occupies the ſpace of *a diſtant* Eagle; *a near* Mole-hill, that of *a diſtant* Mountain. In the perpetration of *Crimes*, there are few perſons, I believe, who would not be more ſhocked at *actually ſeeing* a *ſingle* man *aſſaſſinated* (even taking away the Idea of *perſonal* danger) than they would be ſhocked *in reading the Maſſacre of Paris*.

THE *Wiſe Man*, juſt quoted, wiſhes to ſave us from theſe Errors. He has already informed us—*The thing, that* HATH BEEN, *is that, which* SHALL BE; *and*

* *Eccleſiaſtes*, Chap. vii. v. 10.

THERE

P. III. THERE IS NO NEW THING *under the Sun. Is there any thing whereof it may be ſaid,* SEE, THIS IS NEW? IT HATH BEEN ALREADY *of old time, which* WAS BEFORE US. — He then ſubjoins the Cauſe of this *apparent* Novelty — things *paſt*, when they return, appear *new*, if they are *forgotten*; and things *preſent* will appear ſo, ſhould they too be *forgotten*, when they *return* *.

THIS *Forgetfulneſs* of *what is ſimilar in Events which return* (for in every returning Event *ſuch Similarity exiſts*) is the Forgetfulneſs of a Mind uninſtructed and weak; a Mind ignorant of that great, that PROVIDENTIAL CIRCULATION, which never ceaſes for a moment thro' every part of the Univerſe.

---

* See of the ſame *Eccleſiaſtes, chap. the firſt*, v. 9, and *chap. the ſecond*, v. 16.

IT

C. XV.

It is not like that *Forgetfulneſs*, which I once remember in a man of Letters, who, when at the concluſion of a long life, he found his Memory began to fail, ſaid chearfully—" *Now I ſhall have a* " *pleaſure, I could not have before; that of* " *reading my* OLD BOOKS, *and finding* " *them all* NEW."

THERE was in this *Conſolation* ſomething *philoſophical* and *pleaſing*. And yet perhaps 'tis a *higher* Philoſophy (could we attain it) NOT TO FORGET THE PAST; *but* IN CONTEMPLATION OF THE PAST TO VIEW THE FUTURE, ſo that we may ſay on the *worſt* Proſpects, with a becoming Reſignation, what ENEAS ſaid of old to THE CUMEAN PROPHETESS,

—— *Virgin, no Scenes of Ill*
To me or NEW, *or* UNEXPECTED *riſe;*
I've ſeen 'em ALL; *have ſeen, and long* BEFORE
WITHIN MYSELF *revolv'd 'em in my mind**.

* Æn. VI. 103, 104, 105.

P. III. In such a Conduct, if well founded, there is not only *Fortitude*, but *Piety*: FORTITUDE, which never sinks, from *a conscious Integrity*; and PIETY, which never resists, by referring all to *the Divine Will*.

BUT lest such Speculation, by carrying me *above* my subject, should expose a Writer upon *Criticism* to be himself *crititized*, I shall here conclude these PHILOLOGICAL INQUIRIES.

THE END.

F. Bartolozzi Fec.

APPENDIX

OF

DIFFERENT PIEÇES.

THE FIRST, containing an Account of THE ARABIC MANUSCRIPTS, belonging to THE ESCURIAL LIBRARY in *Spain*.

THE SECOND, containing an Account of THE MANUSCRIPTS OF LIVY in *the ſame Library*.

THE THIRD, containing an Account of THE MANUSCRIPTS OF CEBES, in THE LIBRARY OF THE KING OF FRANCE, at *Paris*.

THE FOURTH, containing ſome Account of LITERATURE IN RUSSIA, and of its *Progreſs* towards being CIVILIZED.

APPENDIX.

PART THE FIRST.

An Account of THE ARABIC MANUSCRIPTS, belonging to *the Escurial Library in Spain.*

THIS Account is extracted from *two fair Folio Volumes*, to *the First* of which Volumes *the Title* is conceived in the following words.

BIBLIOTHECÆ ARABICO-HISPANÆ ESCURALIENSIS, *sive Librorum omnium MSS. quos Arabicè ab auctoribus magnam partem Arabo-Hispanis compositos Bibliotheca Cænobii Escurialiensis complectitur,*

RECENSIO *et* EXPLANATIO:

Opera et Studio MICHAELIS CASIRI,

Syro-Maronitæ, Presbyteri, S. Theologiæ Doctoris, Regis a Bibliothecâ, Linguarumque Orientalium Intérpretatione; CAROLI III. REGIS OPT. MAX. *auctoritate atque auspiciis edita.*

TOMUS PRIOR.

MATRITI.

Antonius Perez de Soto imprimebat

Anno MDCCLX.

This Catalogue is particularly valuable, because not only each Manuscript is enumerated, but its *Age* also and *Author* (when known) are given, together with large *Extracts* upon occasion, both in *the original Arabic*, and in *Latin*.

From the first Volume it appears that the Arabians cultivated every ſpecies of Philosophy and Philology, as alſo (according to their Syſtems) Jurisprudence and Theology.

They were peculiarly fond of Poetry, and paid great honours to thoſe, whom they eſteemed good Poets. Their *earlieſt* Writers were of *this* ſort, ſome of whom (and thoſe much admired) flouriſhed many centuries before the time of *Mahomet*.

The ſtudy of their Poets led them to the Art of Criticism, whence we find in the above Catalogue, not only a multitude of *Poems*, but many works upon *Compoſition*, *Metre*, &c.

We find in the ſame Catalogue Translations of Aristotle and Plato, together with their *Lives*; as alſo Tranſlations of their best Greek Commentators, ſuch as Alexander Aphrodisiensis, Philoponus, and others. We find alſo *Comments of their own*, and *original* Pieces, *formed on the Principles* of the *above Philoſophers*.

There too may be found Translations of Euclid, Archimedes, Apollonius Pergæus, and the other ancient *Mathematicians*, together with their Greek Commentators, and many original Pieces of their own upon *the ſame Mathematical* ſubjects. In the Arithmetical Part they are ſaid to follow Diophantus, from whom they learnt that Al-

gebra,

GEBRA, of which they are *erroneously* thought to have been *the Inventors*.

There we may find also the works of PTOLEMY *translated*, and many original Treatises of *their own* upon the subject of ASTRONOMY.

It appears too, that they Studied with care the important Subject of AGRICULTURE. *One large Work* in particular is mentioned, composed by a *Spanish Arabian*, where every mode of *Culture*, and every species of *Vegetable* is treated; Pasture, Arable, Trees, Shrubs, Flowers, &c. By this work may be perceived (as *the Editor* well observes) *how much better* SPAIN was cultivated in *those* times; and that *some species of Vegetables* were *then* found there, which are *now* lost.

Here are many Tracts on the various Parts of JU-R-ISPRUDENCE; some ancient Copies of the ALCORAN; innumerable COMMENTARIES on it; together with Books of PRAYER, Books of DEVOTION, SERMONS, &c.

Among their *Theological* Works, there are some upon the Principles of THE MYSTIC DIVINITY; and among their *Philosophical*, some upon the Subject of TALISMANS, DIVINATION and JUDICIAL ASTROLOGY.

THE FIRST VOLUME, of which we have been speaking, is elegantly printed, and has *a learned Pre-*

face prefixed by the Editor, wherein he relates what he has done, together with the aſſiſtance he has received, as well from the Crown of *Spain* and its *Miniſters*, as from *learned Men*.

He mentions *a fatal Fire*, which happened at *the Eſcurial*, in the year 1670; when *above three thouſand* of theſe valuable Manuſcripts were deſtroyed. He has in this Volume given an account of *about fourteen hundred*.

THE SECOND VOLUME of this valuable Work, which bears *the ſame* Title with *the Firſt*, was publiſhed at *Madrid*, ten years after it, in the year 1770.

It contains chiefly THE ARABIAN CHRONOLOGERS, TRAVELLERS, and HISTORIANS; and, tho' *national* partiality may be ſometimes ſuſpected, yet, as theſe are accounts given us by the *Spaniſh Arabians themſelves*, there are *many* Incidents preſerved, which other writers could not know, Incidents reſpecting not only *the Succeſſions*, and *the Characters* of the *Arabic-Spaniſh Princes*, but the *Country* and its *Productions*, together with *the Manners*, and *the Literature* of its *then* Inhabitants.

Nor are the Incidents in theſe Volumes *confined* to SPAIN only, many of them relate to *other* Countries, ſuch as the Growth of SUGAR in *Egypt*, the Invention of PAPER there (of which material there are *Manuſcripts* in the *Eſcurial Library* of the year 1180); the uſe of GUNPOWDER, carried not only to the beginning of the fourteenth Century, but even ſo far back (if

we

we can believe it) as to the *seventh* Century; the Decription of MECCA; the *Antiquity* of the ARABIC LANGUAGE, and the practice of THEIR MOST ANTIENT AUTHORS, *to write in verse*; their *Year*, *Months*, *Weeks*, and *Method of Computation*, their Love for POETRY, and RHETORIC, &c.

GREAT HEROES are recorded to have flourished among them, such as *Abdelrahmanus*, and *Abi Amer Almoapheri*.

Abdelrahmanus lived in the beginning of the tenth Century, and *Abi Amer Almoapheri* at its latter end. *The first*, having subdued innumerable Factions and Seditions, reigned at *Corduba* with reputation for fifty years, famed for his love of *Letters*, and his upright administration of *Justice*. *The second*, undertaking the tuition of a young Prince (who was a minor, named *Heschem*) and having restored Peace to a turbid Kingdom, turned his Arms so successfully against its numerous Invaders, that he acquired the honourable name of *Almanzor*, that is, THE DEFENDER. (See Vol. 2d of this Catalogue, pages 37, 49, 50.)

Arabian Spain had too its MEN OF LETTERS, and those in great numbers; some, whose Fame was so extensive, that even *Christians* came to hear them from remote Regions of *Europe*. But this has been already mentioned, p. 394, 395, of these Inquiries.

PUBLIC LIBRARIES (not less than seventy) were established thro' the Country; and noble Benefactions

 they

they were to the Cause of Letters, at a time when *Books*, by being *Manuscripts*, were *so costly* an Article, that few Scholars were equal to the expence of a Collection.

To the Subjects, already treated, were added the Lives of their FAMOUS WOMEN, that is, of *Women* who had been *famous* for their *Literature* and *Genius*.

'Tis somewhat strange, when we read these accounts, to hear it asserted, that *the Religion of these people* was *hostile to Literature*, and this Assertion founded on no better reason, than that *the Turks*, their successors, by being *barbarous* and *ignorant*, had little value for *accomplishments*, *of which they knew nothing*.

These SPANISH ARABIANS also, like their Ancestors *in the East*, were great HORSEMEN, and particularly fond of HORSES. Accounts are preserved both of HORSES and CAMELS; also of their *Coin*; of the *two Races* of *Caliphs*, the *Ommiadæ*, and the *Abbassadæ*; of the first *Arabic* Conqueror of *Spain*, and the Conditions of *Toleration* granted to the *Christians*, whom he had conquered.

It farther appears from these *Arabic* Works, that not only SUGAR, but SILK was known and cultivated IN SPAIN. We read a beautiful Description of GRENADA, and its Environs; as also EPITAPHS of different kinds; some of them approaching to *Attic* Elegance.

When

When that pleasing Liquor COFFEE was first introduced among them, a Scruple arose among *the Devout* (perhaps from feeling its *exhilerating Quality*), whether it was not *forbidden by the* ALCORAN, under the article of WINE. *A Council of Mahometan Divines* was held upon the occasion, and *the Council* luckily *decreed* for *the Legality of its use.* (See Vol. 2d of this Catalogue, p 172, 173.)

The *Concessions* made by *the Arabian Conqueror of Spain* to *the Gothic Prince,* whom he subdued, is a striking Picture of his *Lenity* and TOLERATION. He neither deposed the *Gothic Prince,* nor plundered *his People,* but, on payment of a moderate Tribute, stipulated not to deprive them either of their *Lives* or *Property,* and gave them also their *Churches,* and a *Toleration* for their *Religion.* See this curious Treaty, which was made about the year 712 of the *Christian Æra,* in the *second Vol. of this Catalogue,* p. 106.

When the *Posterity* of these *Conquerors* came in their turn to be conquered, (an Event, which happened *many Centuries afterward)* they did not experience that INDULGENCE, *which had been granted by their Forefathers.*

The conquered Moors (as they were *then* called) were expelled *by thousands*; or, if they ventured to *stay,* were exposed to the Carnage of a merciless *Inquisition*—

—— *pueri, innuptæque puellæ,*
IMPOSITIQUE ROGIS JUVENES *ante ora parentum.*

It appears that many of theſe ARABIC-SPANISH PRINCES were men of *amiable Manners*, and great Encouragers both of *Arts* and *Letters*, while others, on the contrary, were *tyrannic*, *cruel*, and *ſanguinary*.

There were uſually *many* Kingdoms exiſting *at the ſame time*, and theſe on every occaſion *embroiled one with another*; not to mention much *internal Sedition* in each paitioular ſtate.

Like their *Eaſtern* Anceſtors, they appear *not to have ſhared the ſmalleſt Sentiment of* CIVIL LIBERTY; the difference as to *good* and *bad* Goveinment ſeeming to have been *wholly* derived, *according to them*, from the *Worth* or *Pravity* of the Prince, who governed. See p. 385 of theſe Inquiries.

The Reader will obſerve, that the Pages *referring to Facts*, in the *two Hiſtorical Volumes* of theſe Manuſcripts, are *but ſeldom* given, becauſe whoever poſſeſſes thoſe Volumes (and without them any Reference would be uſeleſs) may *eaſily find* every Fact, by referring to the copious and uſeful *Index*, ſubjoined to the *ſecond* Volume, which *Index* goes to the *whole* Work.

A P P E N D I X.

PART THE SECOND.

Concerning the Manuscripts of LIVY, *in the* ESCURIAL LIBRARY.

IT having been often asserted, that AN INTIRE AND COMPLETE COPY OF LIVY was extant in THE ESCURIAL LIBRARY, I requested my Son, in the year 1771 (he being at that time Minister Penipotentiary to the Court of *Madrid)*, to inquire for me, *what Manuscripts of that Author were there to be found.*

He procured me the following accurate Detail from *a learned Ecclesiastic*, DON JUAN DE PELLEGEROS, *Canon of Lerma*, employed by *Monsr.* DE SANTANDER, his *Catholic Majesty's Librarian*, to inspect for this purpose the *Manuscripts* of that valuable *Library.*

The Detail was in *Spanish*, of which the following is a Translation.

Among *the MSS. of* THE ESCURIAL LIBRARY are the following Works of T. LIVY.

1st. THREE LARGE VOLUMES, which contain *so many Decads, the 1st, 3d, and 4th* (one *Decad* in each *Volume)* curiously written on Parchment, or fine Vellum, by *Pedro de Middleburgh*, or of *Zeeland* (as he stiles himself).

The

The Books are truly magnificent, and in the Title and Initials curiously illuminated. They bear *the Arms* of the House of *Borgia*, with a *Cardinal's Cap*, whence it appears that they belonged either to Pope *Callixtus the third*, or to *Alexander the sixth*, when *Cardinals*.

2d. TWO OTHER VOLUMES, written by the same Hand, one of *the first Decad*, the other of *the third*; of the same size, and beauty, as the former. Both have the same *Arms*, and in the last is a Note, which recites: *This Book belongs to D. Juan de Fonseca, Bishop of Burgos.*

3d. ANOTHER VOLUME OF THE SAME SIZE, and something *more antient*, than the former (being of the beginning of the fifteenth Century) containing *the third Decad entire*. This is also well written on Parchment, tho' not so valuable as the former.

4th. ANOTHER OF THE FIRST DECAD, *finely written* on Vellum. At the end is written as follows—*Ex centum voluminibus, quæ ego indies vitæ meæ magnis laboribus hactenus scripsisse memini, hos duos Titi Livii libros Anno Dni.* 1441. *Ego Joañes Andreas de Colonia feliciter, gratia Dei, absolvi*—and at the end of each book—*Emendavi Nicomachus Fabianus.*

In the last leaf of this Book is *a Fragment* either of *Livy himself*, or of some *Pen, capable of imitating him.* It fills the whole leaf, and the Writer says, it was in the Copy, from which he transcribed. It appears to be be a Fragment of the latter times of *the second Punic War*.

5th ANOTHER LARGE VOLUME in Parchment, well written, of the same Century, viz the fifteenth containing *three Decads*—1. *De Urbis initus.* 2. *De Bello Punico* 3. *De Bello Macedonico.* In this *last Decad* is wanting a part of the Book. *This Volume is much esteemed*, being full of *Notes* and *various Readings*, in the hand of *Hieronimo Zunita*, its former possessor.

6th. ANOTHER VERY VALUABLE VOLUME, containing *the first Decad*, equal to the former in the elegance of its Writing and Ornaments. This also belonged to *Hieronimo Zunita*; the age the same.

7th. Lastly, there is ANOTHER OF THE FIRST DECAD also, written on Paper, at the beginning of the fifteenth Century. This contains nothing remarkable.

In all, THERE ARE TEN VOLUMES, and ALL NEARLY OF THE SAME AGE.

Here ends *the Account of the* ESCURIAL MANUSCRIPTS, given us by this *learned Spaniard*, in which Manuscripts we see *there appears no part of* LIVY, *but what was printed in the early Editions.*

The *other* Parts of this Author, which Parts *none of the Manuscripts here recited* give us, were *discovered* and *printed afterwards*.

As to *the Fragment* mentioned in the fourth article, (all of which Fragment is there tranſcribed) it has, *tho' genuine*, no peculiar *rarity*, as it is to be found in all *the latter printed* Editions. See particularly in *Crevier's Edition of Livy, Paris*, 1736, Tome 2d, pages 716, 717, 718, beginning with the words *Raro ſimul hominibus*, and ending with the words *increpatis riſum eſſe*, which is *the whole Extent* of the *Fragment* here exhibited.

From this *Detail* it is evident, that NO INTIRE COPY OF LIVY IS EXTANT IN THE ESCURIAL LIBRARY.

APPENDIX.

PART THE THIRD.

GREEK MANUSCRIPTS OF CEBES, *in* THE LIBRARY OF THE KING OF FRANCE.

THE PICTURE OF CEBES, one of the moſt elegant *Moral Allegories* of *Grecian* Antiquity, is ſo far connected with *the middle Age*, that the ingenious *Arabians* of that time thought it worth tranſlating into ARABIC.

It was alſo tranſlated from *Greek* into *Latin* by *Ludovicus Odaxius*, a learned *Italian*, ſoon after *Greek* Literature revived there, and was publiſhed in the year 1497.

After this it was often printed, ſometimes *in Greek alone*, ſometimes *accompanied* with more modern *Latin* Verſions. But the Misfortune was, that the *Greek* Manuſcripts, from which *the Editors* printed, (that of *Odaxius* alone excepted) were all of them defective in their *End* or *Concluſion*. And hence it followed that *this Work* for *many* years was publiſhed, Edition after Edition, *in this defective manner*.

Had its *End* been loſt, we might have lamented it, as we lament *other* loſſes of the ſame kind. But in the preſent caſe, to the ſhame of Editors, we have THE END PRESERVED, and that not only in *the Arabic Paraphraſe*, and *the old Latin Tranſlation of Odaxius*; but, what is more, even in the ORIGINAL TEXT, as it

ſtands

ſtands in *two excellent Manuſcripts* of *the King of France's Library*.

From theſe MSS it was publiſhed in a neat 12mo. Edition of *Cebes*, by *James Gronovius*, in the year 1689; and after him by the diligent and accurate *Fabricius*, in his *Bibliotheca Græca*, Tom. I. p. 834, 835; and, after *Fabricius*, in a ſmall octavo Edition, by *Thomas Johnſon*, A. M. printed at *London*, in the year 1720.

Whoever reads the Concluſion of this Treatiſe will find ſufficient *internal Evidence* to convince him of *its Authenticity*, both from *the purity of the Language*, and *the Truth*, as well as *Connection of the Sentiment*.

However, *the Manuſcript* authority reſting on nothing better than the perplexed account of that moſt obſcure and affected writer, *James Gronovius*, I procured a ſearch to be made *in the Royal Library at Paris*, if ſuch Manuſcripts were there to be found.

Upon Inſpection of no leſs than FOUR MANUSCRIPTS OF CEBES, preſerved in *that valuable Library*, No. 858, 2992, 1001, 1774, it appeared that in THE SECOND, and in THE THIRD, THE END OF CEBES was PERFECT and INTIRE, after the manner in which *it ſtands in the printed Editions* above mentioned.

The

The End of this ſhort Eſſay is, to prove, that the *Genuineſs of the Concluſion thus reſtored* does not reſt merely on ſuch authority, as that of *James Gronovius*, (for *Fabricius* and *Johnſon* only follow *Him)* but *on the authority of the beſt Manuſcripts, actually inſpected for the purpoſe.*

A P P E N D I X.

PART THE FOURTH.

Some Account of LITERATURE IN RUSSIA, *and of its* Progreſs *towards being* CIVILIZED.

THE vaſt Empire of RUSSIA, extending far into *the North*, both in *Europe* and *Aſia*, 'tis no wonder that, *in ſuch a Country*, its *Inhabitants* ſhould have remained ſo long *uncivilized*. *For Culture of the finer Arts* it is neceſſary there ſhould be *comfortable Leiſure*. But how could ſuch *Leiſure* be found in a Country, where every one had enough to do, to ſupport his family, and to reſiſt the Rigour of an uncomfortable Climate? Beſides this, to make *the finer Arts flouriſh*, there muſt be *Imagination*; and *Imagination* muſt be enlivened by the *Contemplation of pleaſing Objects*; and that *Contemplation* muſt be performed in a manner *eaſy to the Contemplator*. Now, who can contemplate with eaſe, where the Thermometer is often many degrees below *the freezing point?* Or what object can he find *worth contemplating* for thoſe many long months, when all the Water is Ice, and all the Land covered with Snow?

If then the Difficulties were ſo great, how great muſt have been the *Praiſe* of thoſe *Princes* and Legiſlators, who dared attempt *to poliſh mankind* in ſo un-

unpromiſing a Region, and who have been able, by their *perſeverance*, in ſome degree to accompliſh it?

Thoſe, who on this occaſion beſtow the higheſt praiſes upon PETER THE GREAT, praiſe him, without doubt, as he juſtly deſerves. But if they would refer the *Beginning* of this work to *Him*, and much more its *Completion*, they are certainly under a miſtake.

As long ago as the time of our *Edward the 6th*, IVAN BASILOWITZ *adopted Principles of Commerce*, and granted peculiar privileges to the *Engliſh*, on their diſcovery of *a Navigation* to *Archangel*.

A ſad ſcene of ſanguinary Confuſion followed from this period to the year 1612, when a Deliverer aroſe, Prince PAJANKY. He, by unparalleled fortitude, having routed all the Tyrants and Impoſtors of the time, was by the *Bojars* or *Magnates* unanimouſly elected *Czar*. But this Honor He, with a moſt diſintereſted magnanimity, declined *for himſelf*, and pointed out to them MICHAEL FÆDOROWITZ, of the houſe of *Romanoff*, and by his mother's ſide deſcended from *the antient Czars*.

FROM THIS PERIOD we may date the firſt appearances of a *real Civilizing*, and *a Developement* of the Wealth and Power of *the Ruſſian Empire*. MICHAEL reigned thirty-three years. By his wiſdom, and the mildneſs of his character, he reſtored Eaſe and Tranquility to ſubjects, who had been long deprived of thoſe ineſtimable Bleſſings—he encouraged them to *Induſtry*, and gave them an example of the moſt *laudable* behaviour.

His ſon ALEXIUS MICHAELOWITZ was ſuperior to his Father in the Art of *Governing* and ſound *Politics*. He promoted *Agriculture*; introduced into his Empire ARTS AND SCIENCES, of which he was himſelf a lover; publiſhed *a Code of Laws*, ſtill uſed in the Adminiſtration of Juſtice; and greatly improved *his Army*, by mending its diſcipline. This he effected chiefly by the help of *Strangers*, moſt of whom were *Scotch*. *Leſley*, *Gordon*, and *Ker*, are the Names of Families ſtill *exiſting* in this Country.

THEODORE or FÆDOR ſucceeded his Father in 1677. He was of a *gentle Diſpoſition*, and weak Conſtitution; fond of Pomp and Magnificence, and in ſatisfying this paſſion *contributed to poliſh his ſubjects* by the introduction of *foreign Manufactures*, and *Articles of Elegance*, which they ſoon began to adopt and imitate. His delight was in *Horſes*, and he did his country a real ſervice in the beginning and eſtabliſhing of thoſe fine breeds of them in the *Ukraine*, and elſewhere. He reigned ſeven years, and having on his death-bed called his *Bojars* round him, in the preſence of his Brother and Siſter, IVAN and SOPHIA, and of his half Brother PETER, ſaid to them; "*Hear my laſt* "*ſentiments*; *they are dictated by my love for the ſtate*, "*and by my affection for my people—the* BODILY *In*"*firmities of* IWAN *neceſſarily muſt affect his* MENTAL "*Faculties—he is* INCAPABLE *of ruling a Dominion* "*like*

"*like that of* RUSSIA—*he cannot take it amiss, if I re-*
"*commend to you to set him aside, and to let your appro-*
"*bation fall on* PETER, *who to* A ROBUST CONSTI-
"TUTION *joins great* STRENGTH OF MIND, *and*
"*marks of* A SUPERIOR UNDERSTANDING."

Theodore dying in 1682, PETER became *Emperor*, and his brother IVAN remained contented. But SOPHIA, *Iwan's sister*, a Woman of great Ambition, could not bring herself to submit.

The Troubles, which ensued; the imminent Dangers, which PETER escaped; his Abolition of that *turbulent* and *seditious Soldiery*, called *the Strelitz*; *the Confinement* of his half-sister *Sophia* to a Monastery; all these were important Events, which left PETER in the year 1689 with no other competitor, than the mild and easy IWAN; who, dying not many years after, left him SOLE MONARCH OF ALL THE RUSSIAS.

The Acts at home and abroad, in Peace and in War, of *this stupendous and elevated Genius*, are too well known to be repeated by me. PETER adorned his Country with *Arts*, and raised its Glory by *Arms*; he created a *respectable Marine*; founded *St. Petersburgh*, a new Capital, and that from the very ground; rendering it withal one of *the first Cities in Europe* for Beauty and Elegance.

To encourage Letters he formed ACADEMIES, and invited *foreign* Professors not only to PETERSBURGH (his *new* City) but to his *antient* Capital Moscow; at both which places *these Professors* were maintained with *liberal Pensions*.

As a few *Specimens of Literature* from *both* these Cities have recently come to my hand, I shall endeavour to enumerate them, as I think it relative to my subject.

1. PLUTARCHUS περὶ Δυσωπίας, καὶ περὶ Τύχης — *Gr. Lat. cum animadversionibus Reiskii et alior.*— *suas adjecit Christianus Fridericus Matthæi. Typis Universitatis Mosquensis, an.* 1777, 8*vo.*

2. PLUTARCHI *libellus de Superstitione, et Demosthenis Oratio funebris, Gr. Lat. cum notis integris Reiskii et alior.—suas adjecit Christ. Frider. Matthæi—Typis Cæsareæ Mosquensis Universitatis, an.* 1778, 8*vo.*

3. LECTIONES MOSQUENSES, *in two Volumes*, 8vo. *bound together*, and printed at *Leipsic*, an. 1779—they contain various Readings in different Authors, and some entire pieces, all in *Greek*, collected from the Libraries of *Moscow*, and published by *the same* learned Editor.

4. ISOCRATIS, DEMETRII *Cyd. et* MICHAEL GLYCÆ *aliquot Epistolæ, nec non* DION. CHRYSOSTOMI *Oratio*—Græc.—*Typis Universitatis Cæsareæ Mosquensis*—8vo.—*By the same learned Editor.*

5. GLOS-

5. GLOSSARIA GRÆCA MINORA, *et alia Anecdota Græca*—a Work, *consisting of two Parts, contained under one Volume, in a thin Quarto, by the same able Professor, printed at Moscow by the University Types, in the years* 1774 *and* 1775. *A Catalogue of the several pieces in both Parts is subjoined to the end of the second Part—Among the Pieces in the first Part are, Excerpta ex Grammaticâ Niceph. Gregoræ; ex Glossario Cyrilli Alexandrini; Glossarium in Epistolas Pauli; Nomina Mensium;—those of the 2d Part are chiefly Theological.*

6. NOTITIA CODICUM MANUSCRIPTORUM GRÆCORUM BIBLIOTHECARUM MOSQUENSIUM, *cum variis Anecdotis, Tabulis Æneis, Indicibus locupletissimis—edidit Christ. Fridericus Matthæi—Mosquæ, Typis Universitatis, an.* 1776.

This Publication, on *a large Folio Paper,* is as yet *incomplete,* only sixty Pages being printed off. It ends, *Partis primæ Sectionis primæ Finis.*

7. AN ODE to the PRESENT EMPRESS, CATHARINE, in *antient Greek* and *Russian.*

8. AN ODE on *the Birth-day* of CONSTANTINE, second son to the *Grand Duke,* in *antient Greek* and *Russian*—printed at *Petersburgh,* and as we learn from the Title, ἐν τῇ Ἀυτοκρατορικῇ Ἀκαδημίᾳ τῶν Ἐπιςημῶν, *in the Imperial Academy of Sciences.*

9. AN ODE TO PRINCE POTEMKIN, *antient Greek* and *Russian*, and printed (as before) an. 1780.

10. AN ODE, consisting of *Strophe, Antistrophe*, and *Epode, antient Greek* and *Russian*, made in 1779, in honour of THE EMPRESS, THE GREAT DUKE and DUCHESS, and ALEXANDER and CONSTANTINE, their two *Sons*, Grandsons to the Empress.

This *Ode* was *sung* in the *Original Greek by a large number of Voices*, before a numerous and splendid Court in one of the Imperial Palaces.

As I have a Copy of this *Music*, I cannot omit observing, that it is a genuine Exemplar of *the Antient* ANTIPHONA, so well known to *the Church* in very remote ages. On this Plan *two complete Choirs* (each consisting of Trebles, Counters, Tenors, and Bases) *sing against each other*, and *reciprocally answer*; then *unite* all of them; then separate *again*, returning to *the alternate Response*, till *the Whole* at length concludes in *one general Chorus*. The *Music* of this Ode may be called *purely Vocal*, having *no other accompanyment* but that of *an Organ*.

The Composer was no less a man than the celebrated PAESIELLO, so well known at present, and so much admired, both in *Italy* and elsewhere, for Music of a very *different* Character, I mean his truly natural, and pleasing *Burlettas*.

Those,

Thoſe, who are curious to know more of *this Species of Muſic*, may conſult the valuable *Gloſſary* of SPELMAN, under the word ANTIPHONA, and the ingenious *Muſical Dictionary* of ROUSSEAU, under the Word ANTIENNE.

11. A ſhort Copy of *Greek Elegiac Verſes*, printed at *Peterſburgh*, in the year 1780, and addreſt to Prince POTEMKIN, with this *ſingular* Title,

Ἐπίγραμμα ἐπὶ τῆς παμφαοῦς καὶ χαρμοσύνου ΓΟΡΓΕΙΟΦΟΡΙ΄ΑΣ, τῆς κοινοτέρως ΜΑΣΚΑΡΑΔΟΣ καλουμένης, ἣν κ. τ. λ.

Thus *Engliſhed*—*A Poem, on the ſplendid and delightful* FESTIVITY, WHERE THEY WEAR GORGONIAN VISORS; *more commonly called* A MASQUERADE; *which Prince* POTEMKIN *celebrated* &c. &c.

A *better Word* to denote A MASQUERADE could hardly have been *invented*, than the Word here employed, Γοργειοφόρια. In attempting to tranſlate it, that I might expreſs ONE Word, I have been compelled to uſe *many*.

12. A TRANSLATION of *Virgil's Georgics* from *the Latin Hexameters* into GREEK HEXAMETERS, by the celebrated EUGENIUS, famous for his Treatiſe of *Logic*, publiſhed a few years ſince in *antient Greek* at *Leipſic*. He was made an Archbiſhop, but choſe to reſign his dignity. He is now carrying on *this Tranſlation* under the protection of *Prince Potemkin*, but

 has

has as yet gone no farther, than to the end of the *First Georgic.*

The Work is printed on a large Folio Paper, having the *Original* on one side, and the *Translation* on the other. Copious Notes in *Greek* are at the bottom of the several Pages.

Take a short Specimen of the Performance.

Continuo, ventis surgentibus, aut freta ponti
Incipiunt agitata tumescere, et aridus altis
Montibus audiri fragor; aut resonantia longe
Littora misceri, et nemorum increbrescere murmur.

Geor. I. 356.

Ἀυτίκα, ἐγρομένων ἀνέμων, πορθμοῖς ἐπὶ πόντυ
Ἅλς τε σαλευομένη οἰδαίνει, καὶ κορυφαὶ δὲ
Ὄυρεος ἄκραι τραχὺ βοᾶσιν· ἀτὰρ μακρόθεν γε
Ἀκταὶ τ' ἐινάλιοι ῥὰ βρέμονται, κ' ἀιγιαλοὶ τε·
Σμερδαλέου πνοιῆσι δὲ μυκάετ' αἶα καὶ ὥλη.

Of these various *printed* Works, *the first six* were sent me by the learned Scholar above mentioned, *Christianus Fridericus Matthæi*, from *Moscow*; *the* last six I had the honour to receive from Prince *Potemkin* at *Petersburgh.*

Besides the *Printed Books,* the learned Professor at *Moscow* sent me a curious *Latin Narrative* in *Manuscript.*

In

In it he gives an account of a fine *Manufcript* of STRABO, belonging to the *Ecclefiaftical Library* at *Mofcow*—He informs me, this MS. is in *Folio*; contains 427 Leaves; is beautifully written by one, whom he calls a learned and diligent fcribe, at the end of the fifteenth or beginning of the fixteenth Century; and came, as appears by a memorandum in the Manufcript, from *the celebrated Greek Monaftery* at Mount *Athos*.

He adds (which is worth attention) that almoft all the *Greek Manufcripts*, which are now preferved at *Mofcow*, were originally brought *thither* from this *Monaftery*; and that, in the laft Century, by order of *the Emperor Alexius Michäelowitz*, and *the Patriarch Nico*, by means of the *Monk Arfenius*. So early in this Country did a Gleam of Literature fhew itfelf.

He ftrongly *denies* the Fact, that there is any other MS. of STRABO befides this either at *Mofcow*, or at *Peterfburgh*.

Of the *prefent MS.* he has been fo kind as to fend me COLLATIONS, taken from the *firft* and *fecond* Book.

After this he mentions THE UNPUBLISHED HYMN OF HOMER UPON CERES, and THE FRAGMENT of another by the fame Poet UPON BACCHUS; both of which, fince I heard from him, have been publifhed by RUNKENIUS at *Leyden*, to whom *my Correfpondent* had fent them from *the Mofcowan Library*.

He

He has been generous enough to send me Copies of all the Books he has published, for which valuable Donation I take this public opportunity of making my grateful acknowledgments.

With regard to *all the Publications* here mentioned, it is to be observed, that those from PETERSBURGH are said to be printed in *the Imperial Academy of Sciences*; those from MOSCOW, by *the Types of the Imperial University*; each Place *by its stile* indicating its *Establishment.*

In justice TO MY SON, *his Majesty's Minister to the Court of Russia*, it is incumbent upon me to say, that all this Information, and all these Literary Treasures have been procured for me by *his* Help, and thro' *his* Interest.

I must not conclude without observing (tho' perhaps it may be a *Repetition)* that the Efforts to CIVILIZE this country *did not begin from* PETER THE GREAT, but were *much older.* A small Glimmering, like the first Day-break, was seen under Czar IWAN, in the middle of the *sixteenth Century.*

This Dawn of CIVILIZING became more conspicuous *a Century afterwards*, under Czar ALEXIUS MICHAELOWITZ; of whom, as well as of his son THEODORE or FÆDOR we have spoken already.

But under THE GREAT PETER it burst forth, with all the splendor of a Rising Sun, and (if I may

be

be permitted to continue my Metaphor) has continued ever ſince to aſcend towards its Meridian.

More than fifty years have paſt ſince the Death of PETER; during which period, with very little exception, *this vaſt Empire has been governed by* FEMALE SOVEREIGNS ONLY. All of them have purſued more or leſs the Plan of their great Predeceſſor, and none of them more, than THE ILLUSTRIOUS PRINCESS, who *now* reigns.

And ſo much for LITERATURE IN RUSSIA, and for ITS PROGRESS TOWARDS BEING CIVILIZED.

ADVERTISEMENT.

IT was proposed, as mentioned in p. 41 *of this Work, to have joined a few Notes to the Pieces contained in the preceding Appendix; but, the Work growing larger than was expected, the Notes, as not being essentially Parts of it, have been omitted.*

One Omission however we beg to supply, because it has happened thro' Inadvertence. Besides the Arabic *Translations from* the Greek, *mentioned in the Appendix, Part the First, there are also Translations of* HIPPOCRATES, GALEN, *and* the old Greek Physicians, *whom* the Arabians, *as they translated, illustrated with Comments, and upon whose Doctrines they formed many Compositions of their own, having been remarkably famous for their Study and Knowlege of* MEDICINE.

I N D E X.

We here repeat, what we have said already, that THE TWO CAPITAL LETTERS, A *and* B. *which occur in this Index, denote* THE TWO VOLUMES: *for example.* A 112, *denotes page* 112, *of* THE FORMER VOLUME; B 337, *denotes page* 337 *of* THE LATTER *Volume*; *and so, in other instances.*

A.

Accuracy,

INDEX.

I N D E X.

ARI-

INDEX.

BACON,

I N D E X.

C.

I N D E X.

D.

F.

Friend,

H.

K.

INDEX.

L.

Liberality.

N.

SADE

O.

PRI-

Q.

R.

S.

I N D E X.

thro'

FINIS.

Lightning Source UK Ltd.
Milton Keynes UK
UKHW010302080119
335175UK00009B/257/P